W9-DAE-638

EXPERIMENTING WITH THE TRUTH

EXPERIMENTING
WITH THE TRUTH

Prabhuji

EXPERIMENTING WITH THE TRUTH
BY PRABHUJI

Copyright © 2023
First edition

Printed in India

All rights reserved. None of the information contained in this book may be reproduced, republished, or re-disseminated in any manner or form without the prior written consent of the publisher.

Published by Prabhuji Mission
Website: prabhuji.net

Avadhutashram
PO Box 900
Cairo, NY, 12413
USA

Painting on the cover by Prabhuji:
"Mitzpeh"
Acrylic on canvas, New York
Canvas Size: 12" x 16"

Library of Congress Control Number: 2021906554
ISBN-13: 978-1-945894-32-9

CONTENTS

ॐ अज्ञानतिमिरान्धस्य ज्ञानाञ्जनशलाकया ।
चक्षुरुन्मीलितं येन तस्मै श्रीगुरवे नमः ॥

oṁ ajñāna-timirāndhasya
jñānāñjana-śalākayā
cakṣur unmīlitaṁ yena
tasmai śrī-gurave namaḥ

Salutations unto that holy Guru who, applying the ointment [medicine] of [spiritual] knowledge, removes the darkness of ignorance of the blinded ones [unenlightened] and opens their eyes.

This book is dedicated, with deep gratitude and eternal respect, to the holy lotus feet of my beloved masters His Divine Grace Avadhūta Śrī Brahmānanda Bābājī Mahārāja (Guru Mahārāja) and His Divine Grace Bhakti-kavi Atulānanda Ācārya Mahārāja (Gurudeva).

INTRODUCTION

The story of my life is nothing more than a long journey, from what I believed myself to be to what I truly am. It is an authentic inner and outer pilgrimage. It is a tale of transcending what is personal and universal, partial and total, illusory and real, apparent and true. My life is a flight beyond what is temporary and eternal, darkness and light, humanity and divinity. This story is not public but profoundly private and intimate.

Only what begins, ends; only what starts, finishes. One who lives in the present is neither born nor dies, because what has no beginning has no end.

I am a disciple of a seer, an enlightened being, and somebody who is nobody. I was initiated in my spiritual childhood by the moonlight. A seagull who loved flying more than anything else in life inspired me. In love with the impossible, I crossed the universe obsessed with a star. I have walked infinite paths, following the footsteps of those who could see.

Like the ocean that longs for water, I sought my home within my own house.

I am a simple intermediary who shares his experience with others. I am not a guide, coach, teacher, instructor, educator, psychologist, enlightener, pedagogue, evangelist, rabbi, *posek halacha*, healer, therapist, satsangist, psychic, leader, medium, savior, or guru. I am only a traveler whom you can ask for directions. I will gladly show you a place where everything calms upon arrival, a place beyond the sun and the stars, beyond your desires and longings, beyond time and space, beyond concepts and conclusions, and beyond everything that you believe you are or imagine that you will be.

I am just a whim or perhaps a joke from the sky and the only mistake of my beloved spiritual masters.

Aware of the abyss that separates revelation and our works, we live in a frustrated attempt to faithfully express the mystery of the spirit.

I paint sighs, hopes, silences, aspirations, and melancholies, inner landscapes, and sunsets of the soul.

I am a painter of the indescribable, inexpressible, and indefinable of our depths. Or maybe I just write colors and paint words.

Since childhood, little windows of paper captivated my attention; through them, I visited places, met people, and made friends. Those tiny *maṇḍalas* were my true elementary school, high school, and college. Like skilled teachers, these *yantras* have guided me through contemplation, attention, concentration, observation, and meditation.

Like a physician studies the human body, or a lawyer studies laws, I have dedicated my entire life to the study of myself. I can say with certainty that I know what resides and lives in this heart.

It is not my intention to convince anyone of anything. I do not offer theology or philosophy, nor do I preach or teach, I simply think out loud. The echo of these words may lead you to the infinite space of peace, silence, love, existence, consciousness, and absolute bliss.

Do not search for me. Search for yourself. You do not need me or anyone else, because the only thing that really matters is you. What you yearn for lies within you, as what you are, here and now.

I am not a merchant of rehashed information, nor do I intend to do business with my spirituality. I do not teach beliefs or philosophies. I only speak about what I see and just share what I know.

Avoid fame, for true glory is not based on public opinion but on what you really are. What matters is not what others think of you, but your own appreciation of who you are.

Choose bliss over success, life over reputation, and wisdom over information. If you succeed, you will know not only admiration but also true envy. However, jealousy is mediocrity's tribute to talent and an open acceptance of one's own inferiority.

I advise you to fly freely and never be afraid of making mistakes. Learn the art of transforming your mistakes into lessons. Never blame others for your faults: remember that taking complete responsibility for your life is a sign of maturity. When you fly, you learn that what matters is not touching the sky but the courage to spread your wings. The higher you rise, the smaller and less significant the world looks. As you walk, sooner or later you will understand that every search begins and ends in you.

Your unconditional well-wisher,
Prabhuji

On what authority do you base your teachings?

The authority of my words comes from me, from what I am; it is not derived from books or from other human beings, but from experience. What I say may at times resonate with your beliefs and at times conflict with them. My words, however, need no evidence to prove their validity, because I only speak about what happens within me. My descriptions will not always agree with your Bhagavad Gita, Vedas, New Testament, and Koran. In the end, all authority comes from ourselves. Even if we accept the words of the scriptures as absolute, we are the ones who give validity to what we consider sacred scriptures.

הָרוֹצֶה שֶׁיְקַבֵּל עָלָיו עוֹל מַלְכוּת שָׁמַיִם שְׁלֵמָה יִפָּנֶה, וְיִטּוֹל
יָדָיו, וְיַנִּיחַ תְּפִילָיו, וְיִקְרָא קְרִיאַת שְׁמַע, וְיִתְפַּלֵּל, וְזוֹ הִיא
מַלְכוּת שָׁמַיִם שְׁלֵמָה.

(תלמוד בבלי, ברכות י"ד, ב'- ט"ו, א')

> Rabbi Yochanan further said, "One who wishes to accept upon himself the complete yoke of Heaven should evacuate himself, wash his hands, put on *t'fillin*, recite the *Sh'ma*, and say his prayers. This is the complete acceptance of the Yoke of Heaven."
> (*Talmud Bavli, Brachot*, 14b–15a)

Are we not the ones who grant supremacy to our popes, priests, imams, lamas, and gurus? How can a verse from a scripture decide if I am satisfied or not? How can someone other than me determine that I am tired? What authority does a religious leader have to decree if I am in love? We are the sole authority of our internal world.

Institutionalized religion preaches the supremacy of an external authority. This strips believers of authority and gives it to scriptures and prophets. But blindly accepting authority destroys all searching and, therefore, any possibility of finding, discovering, or unveiling. Truth cannot be acquired through some external intermediary; it is extremely delicate and withers when passed on. For one to truly learn rather than merely accumulate secondhand knowledge that has been passed down, it is necessary to leave out any external authority. You are authoritative when you speak out of your own experience. You act with authenticity if your actions originate in what you really are.

Truth does not flow through professional declaimers who simply recite words. Millions of preachers, instructors, and scholars go around the world recounting the experiences of others with well-documented ignorance. Someone can have an excellent memory, but that does not make them an authority.

Absolute authority belongs to Truth alone. Only the words of someone who is Truth itself are authoritative. Reality can flow through those who have emptied themselves, such as Moses, Samuel, the Baal Shem Tov, Rabbi Nachman of Breslov, Alter Rebbe, Rashi, Buddha, Jesus, Lao-Tze, and Kabir. Since such discourse does not stem from the mind, it cannot be considered mere "words," but is speech from a plane that transcends words.

רַבִּי בָא בַּר כֹּהֵן בְּשֵׁם רַבִּי יוּדָה בֶּן פָּזִי: תֵּדַע לָךְ שֶׁחֲבִיבִים
דִּבְרֵי סוֹפְרִים מִדִּבְרֵי תוֹרָה.

(תלמוד ירושלמי, מסכת ברכות, פרק א')

Rabbi Ba, son of Cohen, [said] in the name
of Rabbi Yuda, son of Pazi, "You should
know that the words of the *Sofrim* (sages, the
first exponents of the oral law) are preferable
over the words of the Torah (Bible)."

(*Talmud Yerushalmi, Brachot,* Chapter 1)

Muhammad's teachings are authoritative, not the
words of Muslim preachers. The message of the Ba'al
Shem Tov has authority, not the words of a professional
preacher. The teachings of Śaṅkara are filled with
authority, not those of pandits. The words of Krishna
are bona fide, not those of the Vaishnava missionaries.
The teachings of enlightened masters have authority,
not the preaching of religious propagandists.

Only those who have seen the Truth can talk about
it. Light flows through a *tattva-darśin*, a "seer of the
Truth."

tad-viddhi praṇipātena
paripraśnena sevayā
upadekṣyanti te jñānaṁ
jñāninas tattva-darśinaḥ

Try to learn the Truth by approaching a
spiritual master. Inquire submissively and
render service to the master. Self-realized

souls can impart knowledge unto you because they have seen the Truth.

(Bhagavad Gita, 4.34)

I am not against accepting an enlightened master, because the other option is to surrender to the mind. The ego of one who does not submit to the authority of Truth inevitably takes control. But even if we accept a master, we are the ones who grant him or her authority over our lives. If we forget this, we will convert the guru into a simple external authority.

יְהוֹשֻׁעַ בֶּן פְּרַחְיָה וְנִתַּאי הָאַרְבֵּלִי קִבְּלוּ מֵהֶם. יְהוֹשֻׁעַ בֶּן פְּרַחְיָה אוֹמֵר, עֲשֵׂה לְךָ רַב, וּקְנֵה לְךָ חָבֵר, וֶהֱוֵי דָן אֶת כָּל הָאָדָם לְכַף זְכוּת.

(פרקי אבות א׳, ו׳)

... Joshua the son of Perachia would say, 'Make for yourself a master, acquire for yourself a friend, and judge every man on the side of merit.

(*Pirkei Avot,* 1.6)

The freedom to decide always comes from you. As Krishna states:

iti te jñānam ākhyātaṁ
guhyād guhya-taraṁ mayā
vimṛśyaitad aśeṣeṇa
yathecchasi tathā kuru

Thus I have explained to you the most
confidential of all knowledge. Deliberate on
this fully and then do what you wish to do.
(Bhagavad Gita, 18.63)

In fact, by surrendering to a realized being, you
do not accept the authority of a body-mind complex
but of the Truth expressed in that being. Only those
who have ceased to be someone can become masters.
The authority of one who has realized the authenticity
is not foreign to what you are. It cannot be considered
external, because it does not come from the master's
personality but from nearness to the Truth.

Truth is infectious, and we can catch it if we come
close to an element infected by it. It cannot be taught, only
transmitted... and the difference is immense! Teaching
implies words; transmission occurs in silence. Teaching is
of the mind; transmission is of the heart. Truth cannot be
found in courses, retreats, lectures, or organizations; nor
does it reside in the information accumulated through
external experiences. Truth is revealed by recognizing
our mental content and consciousness. The revelation of
the light of Truth comprises the recognition of our reality,
of our authenticity.

It is impossible to have Truth delivered to our house
like a pizza. Nothing and no one can bring reality to
our illusion, so we must rise up to the Truth ourselves.
We cannot make it to the summits of the Himalayas by
descending into the valleys. If we wish to reach the peak,
we must leave the valley and climb the mountain.

I have often heard you speak of freedom. What do you mean by freedom?

Most people believe that freedom means escaping from life's limitations. They confuse freedom with overcoming oppression: the prisoner wants to be free from jail; the slave, from the master; the depressed person, from sadness; and the sick, from pain. Freedom, however, is not the same thing as emancipation or release, even though they are synonymous in the dictionary. Emancipation means releasing oneself *from* something. Freedom, on the other hand, does not entail any kind of escape; it cannot be dependent on anything.

Release from slavery is born from slavery and, therefore, remains an integral part of it. Its very existence depends on slavery, and thus, it is not exempt from oppression. The same happens with relief from hunger or a toothache: it is just a desire to exchange an intolerable situation for a pleasant one; that is, to exchange uncomfortable conditions for more promising ones. It is merely a reaction against what we wish to be released from. It is not a pursuit of freedom but an escape from certain circumstances. Release from poverty is not related to freedom but rather to money. Release from disease has nothing to do with freedom but rather with medicine, pain, and hospitals; and release from slavery, with shackles and prison cells.

Some live their lives running away from freedom because they are afraid to accept the responsibility. They are content with just imagining what freedom is and blaming others for their oppression. The people of Israel were released from captivity when they left Egypt, but they only became free on Mount Sinai, when they accepted the responsibility of receiving the Torah.

In his essay *Two Concepts of Liberty*, Isaiah Berlin makes a difference between positive and negative freedom, both clearly reflected in the Universal Declaration of Human Rights. The negative is "freedom from something," meaning the absence of obstacles to action. The positive is "freedom for something," the possibility of choosing the actions that accomplish our goals.

The idea of freedom most people have is limited to these two types: positive and negative; freedom from something and freedom to do something. The first is related to the past, the second to the future. However, both are merely psychological reactions and superficial types of emancipation. They go after our mental projections, not reality. Real freedom cannot be conceived from within the limitations of the mind, but only when the content of the mind is transcended.

Reasoning is nothing but a response to our conditioning, from the experiences accumulated in our memory. Thus, thought is inevitably chained to this heavy load of accumulated experiences.

We are not free from our psychological limitations. According to Karl Marx, the economic structure of capitalist society defines how we interpret the world. As victims of this "false class consciousness," we necessarily interpret the world from a viewpoint determined by our social class. Marx believed that the only way to disentangle ourselves from the limitations of this perspective and to be free was by understanding dialectical materialism and adopting socialism, which, of course, is highly debatable. As a matter of fact, political freedom does not exist, because it only has meaning in relation to others. Various political movements have tried to impose their own concept of freedom and turned into totalitarian and oppressive regimes.

We are conditioned not just by capitalism but by society as a whole and all that it implies. Likewise, we indisputably lack the psychological freedom needed to access reality. Expressions such as "freedom of thought" or "freedom of worship" are nothing more than verbal stimulants that activate our conditioning. All of our ideas and concepts about other people, about the world, about life, and therefore about freedom, stem from our psychological limitations. Only by transcending this conditioning will we gain an objective perception of reality. Without a clear perception, aspiration for freedom is impossible.

Authentic freedom has an existence of its own. It is independent of everything and has no cause or motive. Absolute freedom simply *is*. The Sanskrit term *mokṣa* means "freedom." Those who aspire to freedom are called *mumukṣu*, ones who aspire to the authentic freedom that flourishes from consciousness.

True freedom is not physical, mental, economic, or sexual. If we found ourselves alone in the desert, a suitcase with ten million dollars would not increase our freedom one bit. Authentic freedom does not belong to objective, temporal, and therefore, illusory reality. Freedom is subjective and belongs to eternal and infinite consciousness. Since it is an intrinsic quality of our reality, freedom cannot be given or taken away from us; it is inherent in our true nature. Nothing and nobody external to us can liberate or suppress us. In fact, we do not even have the freedom to renounce our freedom. It is possible to oppress the body or the mind, but consciousness can never be limited. Meditation is the only opportunity to recognize freedom without any kind of limitations. Only within the depths of our interior are we free from the body, mind, emotions, and all that we believe ourselves to be. The New Testament points this out: "Then you will know the Truth, and the Truth will set you free" (John, 8:32).

Absence of freedom means lack of consciousness. We are as free as we are conscious. Such freedom is not "from something," nor "for something," but simply to be what we are. Freedom is a return to the state of original and pure consciousness. Our authenticity is freedom, which is the divine source and origin of any virtue.

When we transcend the relative, the Absolute is revealed; when we go beyond falsehood, reality is unveiled; when the illusory and temporal is transcended, Truth is recognized; and when we go one step beyond the ego, freedom is discovered. Only the recognition of Truth will allow us to transcend the fetters of illusion and know who we really are.

When talking about freedom,
you mention responsibility.
Isn't responsibility an
obstacle to freedom?

To answer your question, we need to understand four factors: freedom, responsibility, control, and discipline.

Generally, people think that freedom is the ability to do whatever they want without any limitations. They believe that freedom means choosing and deciding without restrictions. This notion, however, does not recognize the responsibility that freedom entails. As the Argentinian writer Jorge Bucay said, "The true seeker grows and learns and discovers that he or she is always primarily responsible for whatever happens." Bucay is right: the freedom to make conscious decisions always comes with responsibility. Freedom is responsibility, and vice versa. George Bernard Shaw said, "Liberty means responsibility. That is why most men dread it." Responsibility means consciously accepting the consequences of our choices.

We must understand that a conditioned mind lacks freedom. Such a mind may dream of being free, but it only responds according to its conditioning. Freedom, however, is not about responding indiscriminately to all of our mental and emotional demands. Jean-Jacques Rousseau said: "Man is born free, and everywhere he is in chains." As long as our yearning for liberation is born from oppression, we will seek to escape its bonds rather than free ourselves. We often think that if the oppressing element vanishes, we will be free. Hence our attention is focused on the chains, on what we desire to be liberated from, rather than on freedom itself.

Now we should understand what responsibility is. Many people link it to duty: we think that being responsible means fulfilling our obligations diligently.

Furthermore, we hold ourselves accountable if we fail to meet them. This idea is both incomplete and superficial. The deeper meaning of the term *responsibility*, which comes from the Latin *responsum*, is the ability to respond. If we live like sleepwalkers, we cannot respond properly.

Responsibility means responding appropriately to life's events with all our capacity. If we were all responsible, we would not need laws, judges, or policemen. But since society is made up of immature people, governments resort to control to maintain order. A higher state of consciousness would allow us to adequately respond to life and to make this world a paradise.

Every moment and situation is a call and requires a response that satisfies the demands of life. Unfortunately, many such invitations remain unanswered because we are not present. Due to our conditioning, we are stuck in memories of the past or hopes for the future. We are absent from the present and from reality. We suffer because we cannot adequately respond to life's invitations. There is no one in the universe who can respond as we would. But in order to respond in our own style, we have to transcend conditioning and regain the ability to listen.

The Sanskrit term *śravaṇa* means "to listen." Listening with precision requires silence, as it is impossible to talk and simultaneously perceive what someone is saying. As silence intensifies, attention sharpens. The inner stillness that the *śravaṇa* requires is not absence of noise but of preconceived ideas, concepts, conclusions, and mental fluctuations. Surely, the first step on the retroprogressive path is cultivating receptivity. Cultivate listening: when you have a doubt related to your health, listen to your body. When you are not sure what direction you should take in life, listen carefully to existence deep within your heart. Those who cultivate the art of receptive and alert listening find silence and peace. Only if we are consciously present in the now will the ability to respond flourish in us. Inner responsibility is born when we are attuned to the present. Responding appropriately requires being in tune with the now.

Responsibility is discipline. By learning something we respond, and by responding we learn. To be able to ride a bicycle, for example, we need to learn how to respond. If the bicycle tilts to the left, we lean to the right, and vice versa. With a lot of attention, observation, and presence, we respond to the various situations that the learning process requires. It is impossible to separate responsibility from learning. Responsibility is discipline; responding is learning.

When we notice our own unacceptable, undesirable, or indecent inclinations, we often try to repress them by exerting control. Yet, this resistance is still an egotistic assessment for our personal convenience. Even our ambition for freedom falls into the same category. The ego may be controlled, but it will remain an ego nonetheless. This control, or misunderstood discipline, does not help us eliminate our inclinations but only repress them. Repressive control hardens us and creates a conflict between "what I am" and "what I should be", between "what I see" and "what I should be seeing."

Hiding our internal conflict, we become atrophied and lose agility. Although repressed and restricted, these undesirable inclinations continue to live and move within us.

> You are still not free, you seek freedom.
> Your seeking made you sleep-deprived and over-awake.
> You aspire to the free heights, your soul thirsts for the stars. But your wicked instincts also thirst for freedom.
> Your wild dogs want to get free; they bark with joy in their cellar when your spirit contrives to liberate all prisons.
> To me you are still a prisoner who plots his freedom. Alas, the soul of such prisoners grows clever, but also deceptive and rotten.
> The one who is free of spirit must still purify himself. Much prison and mold is left in him: his eyes must still become pure.
> (*Thus Spoke Zarathustra*, Friedrich Nietzsche)

Control paralyzes certain inclinations and creates habits. It turns living beings into robots and destroys intelligence and creativity. Control shrinks us; it impels us to perform specific actions and aggravates our conditioning. Clearly, freedom is not acquired through control, because we cannot be free within our conditioning, whether positive or negative. To reach freedom and responsibility, sensitivity is required. Sensitivity is not cultivated by control but with discipline.

Therefore, it is necessary to separate the terms discipline and control because, although they sound similar, they are completely different.

The word *discipline* comes from the Latin term *discipulus*, which, in turn, is derived from *discere* or *disco*, i.e., "one who learns" or "one who has an aptitude for learning." People relate discipline to control, but these two are totally different. Control is a series of laws, rules, and regulations, while discipline is born of understanding and awareness. Many think that it is necessary to dominate animal nature; yet, control is also part of the egoic phenomenon. Control assaults our nature, whereas discipline is spontaneous and blossoms out of consciousness.

Free beings, and therefore responsible beings, require no control, for they are aware of their own needs and those of others. Those who are unconscious and irresponsible have to be controlled because they lack the sensitivity to respond to existence. Conscious beings are disciplined but free of control. They live awake like seagulls flying high, in total freedom, without laws or rules.

Now we shall examine how freedom, discipline, and responsibility are related. Discipline, in its true meaning, is learning, not in the sense of accumulating knowledge or information, but in the sense of perceiving and observing what is, as it is. In order to learn, it is necessary to completely free ourselves from all accumulated information. Otherwise, instead of observing what is, we will project what we know on what we are learning. We will not observe reality, but only what we grasp according to our conditioning. The freedom to perceive and to observe is essential for learning. If we wish to study ourselves, we must get rid of all beliefs, concepts, and conclusions about what we are. This kind of learning is responsibility, because it is a response to existence.

Society confuses control with discipline, because it maintains a semblance of order by controlling unconscious people. Unlike imposed order, discipline reveals the harmony of life. Trying to control our thoughts will not help us create inner order. Inner harmony can be discovered only by observing our mental activity.

From within the known, our reaction will always be mechanical. Only when we become free from all conditioning and respond to the call of existence will we act responsibly. Once we transcend memory, we will respond consciously. To be responsible is to be disciplined. An irresponsible being has to be motivated or impelled through control; only those who are responsible can learn.

No, dear friend, responsibility is not an obstacle to your freedom. Responsibility and discipline are implicit in freedom.

Dear Prabhuji, can freedom be misused?

Unlike slavery, freedom can be misused. It is said that to err is human; hence, anyone can use freedom inappropriately. Slavery, on the other hand, can never be misused. Prisoners are deprived of their ability to choose. Slaves cannot misuse their captivity. When freedom is taken away, misjudgment is also impeded. Freedom entails choice and, therefore, the possibility of going in the wrong direction.

For Aristotle, human beings are rational creatures, but their instincts remain animalistic. Even though they have the faculty of reason, they share their instinctive desires with the animal kingdom. According to Descartes, nature pursues its own goals through animals, which act in accordance with their instincts. Just as it is for animals, most of human behavior is motivated by certain instinctive demands. Since only human beings have access to freedom, only they can misuse it. Their freedom entails moral responsibility. In his famous work *Existentialism is a Humanism*, Jean-Paul Sartre wrote: "Man is condemned to be free." The French philosopher thought that freedom was inherent to the human condition and that human beings were responsible for using it. Mankind is the only species capable of being free and of mitigating, sublimating, and transcending its desires.

For Friedrich Nietzsche, human beings are not the final goal but only a phase in a process leading to greatness. Humanity represents an evolutionary bridge between the beast and the overman.

> Mankind is a rope fastened between animal and overman—a rope over an abyss [...]

What is great about human beings is that
they are a bridge and not a purpose: what is
lovable about human beings is that they are
a *crossing over* and a *going under.*
(*Thus Spoke Zarathustra*, Friedrich Nietzsche)

Nietzsche is right. Unlike animals, human beings
are not complete. Chickens are born as chickens and
cannot change their nature; the life of an animal is a
finalized process. Human beings, on the other hand,
are "under construction." They are a process stretching
between animal and divine nature, between the
instinctive and the transcendental essence. They move
from unconsciousness to consciousness. They are a rope
strung over an abyss into which they can fall if they
misuse their freedom. They can hit the bottom or reach
divine heights, lift themselves up or tear themselves
down, transcend the mind or fall under it.

The singularity of human beings lies in the fact
that they are not born completed and programmed.
Understanding and accepting this freedom turns our
life into a challenge to complete ourselves.

In the Bible we read: "And God said, 'Let us make
man in our image, after our likeness'." (Genesis, 1:26).
However, many verses declare that God is unique,
for example: "… the Lord is God in heaven above and
on the earth below. There is no other." (Deuteronomy,
4:39). So, how can a single God speak in the plural? With
whom does God speak when He says "let us make"?
Who else joins God in the process of creation? If I say to
someone, "Let's dance," they will understand that I am

inviting them to be an active participant in the dance. When God says "let us make," regardless of whom He is addressing, He is clearly referring to another active participant in creation. In fact, He was speaking to the first man, Adam. God created all creatures, but unlike animals and the rest of creation, human beings are not just His work but a partnership between Him and them. By saying "let us make man," God tells Adam that His creation, in fact, is ours. He tells us that even though He created us, it is our duty to continue. By completing ourselves, we are taking part in the divine work. Human beings are not a finalized creation but architects of their own destiny. Their essence is freedom. To deny this is to rob them of their essence.

The misuse of freedom is obviously possible because humans can err. Freedom implies that we can make right or wrong decisions. If we were not able to choose incorrectly, we would not be truly free. Naturally, going down is tempting, because it requires less effort and energy than going up.

Freedom is a challenge that implies responsibility. We are intimidated by the risk of erring. That is why most people choose to place their lives in the hands of others. We blame others for our defeats and failures. We criticize our parents for the way they raised us, and we put spiritual masters in charge of our enlightenment. Afraid of making mistakes, we live according to rules decreed in a sacred book or by a guru. We renounce our freedom to keep from making a wrong decision. If we were not afraid to accept responsibility over our lives, society would be full of enlightened beings.

Every day we would see beings such as Krishna, Jesus, and Buddha. However, we have been intimidated for centuries, both by politicians and religious leaders. Politicians have frightened us with poverty, hunger, and war, and religious leaders have done so with hell. Fear has been cultivated in order to dominate the masses, and that is why there are so few enlightened beings. Mahatma Gandhi said, "Freedom is not worth having if it does not connote freedom to err. It is beyond my comprehension how human beings, be they ever so experienced and able, can delight in depriving other human beings of that precious right."

Free beings can make mistakes but never fail, because errors teach them and contribute to their development. As Carl Jung said, "In this way, the last thing I want to tell you, dear friends, is the following: live your life as best you can, even if your life is based on an error, because life must be consumed, and truth is reached by error." Instead of defeats, errors are an integral part of our evolutionary learning process.

It is not my intention to restrict anyone's freedom but to help understand it. Having comprehended what freedom is, make your own decisions. Do not be afraid to make mistakes, because in the long process of development, errors are as important as successes. The important thing is not to avoid falling down but to understand the lesson. In the school of life, we learn from both our defeats and triumphs.

I think that your teachings could benefit many people if they were spread on a larger scale. Why don't you try to reach more people? Why is your organization so small? Why not to enlarge it and expand to other countries?

I live faithfully according to what existence dictates. It is not my intention to preach or to persuade anyone to walk alongside me, a mere servant. My love for the heights has awarded me a life of solitude in divine company. I do not consider myself a guru, a rabbi, or a master, even though I respect the opinion of those who see me as such. I equally accept flattery, criticism, glorification, and defamation. I feel more at ease when I am called a communicator, a writer, or someone who sings in the shower and does not expect anything to come of it. I carry on with my work without expecting that a crowd of followers and adepts will perpetuate my words. I do not aspire to make myself eternal through some ideology or method. Too many theologies and philosophies have ended up being obstacles in the evolutionary path of many people. They begin as bridges that are meant to unite, but become walls that separate and hinder development.

I am not one of your typical "life coaches" who do not evolve because they are too busy changing others. I do not wish to evangelize, because the role of a preacher or missionary does not suit me. I do not have enough ego to take on the role of the savior of humanity, neither do I have the stomach to bear the nausea it causes me, because no one has harmed humanity as cruelly as its bloodthirsty saviors. No one has inflicted more pain and suffering on people than their liberators. God save us from our saviors!

All enlightened beings have left footprints along the way. The echo of these steps is canonized, interpreted, commented on, and finally presented as their message to society. Such efforts to organize Truth inevitably diminish its freshness and nutritional value. Many truths have been ruined by attempts to institutionalize them, and turned into creeds to convince others. But Truth is not meant to be institutionalized, because it belongs to the realm of individuality. Organization prevents people from revealing the Truth that lies in their heart of hearts. In this process, the transcendental experience becomes a simple ideology. What happens in an individual's deepest intimacy becomes a social phenomenon. Many people have tried to institutionalize the Truth. Although they may have had good intentions, the results were disastrous. Efforts to expand their organizations brought about institutionalized religion, which then buried truths under mountains of interpretations, dogmas, rules, laws, and regulations. The Truth has been stripped of its spirituality and become more like politics.

There are those who prefer to ignore their own development and dedicate themselves to the "benefit of humanity." They teach what they do not know, talk about what they are unfamiliar with, and describe what they do not see. When the individuality of an enlightened being is systematized, authentic learning is replaced by imitation. The main focus becomes public dissemination and preserving the system. In the process of large-scale preaching, the original vision is changed. The teachings of Jesus, Buddha, Muhammad, Moses, Lao-Tze, and many others have been transformed into simple "isms." These "isms" are like corpses of someone who once breathed, palpitated, danced, and loved; they are nothing but beautiful mausoleums commemorating spiritual giants who walked our earth.

It is said that one day, the devil and his assistant were walking down the street. They saw a man stop along the way, pick something up from the ground, and put it in his pocket. The assistant asked, "What did this man find?" The devil answered, "A piece of Truth." The assistant then exclaimed, "But this is very bad for us!", to which the devil replied, "Don't worry, I'll let him create an organization."

As an organization develops, concessions to the original message are made for the group's benefit. The institution's security and well-being take precedence over its founding principles. Since the organization is primary, the initial message is relegated to something secondary. Eventually, all religious institutions that perpetuate themselves do so at the cost of the original principles. The organization remains, but the message perishes. We cannot be liberated by surrendering to an organized spiritual cause. I think it is crazy to believe that by joining an organization I could be saved or that by adhering to a certain belief I will reach paradise. Such organizations become obstacles for individuals' development and evolution.

Of course, I have agreed to a small organization dedicated to printing my books and filming my talks. The purpose of our organization is not spiritual but entirely practical. Born out of logistical needs, it does not strive to attract adepts.

It is time for society to mature. Humanity clearly needs help, but it is not an easy task to spread teachings on a large scale without distorting them. As for me, I do not aspire to expand my organization, but to express myself. I address the individual and not the masses. Humanity does not need more spiritual institutions but more individuals who seek Truth, love, and freedom. It needs beings who are interested in realizing consciousness and who are eager to discover their own authenticity. The world is plagued with religious organizations that venerate the past and worship those who experienced divinity centuries ago. They spread messages based on a second-hand retelling of what happened to an enlightened being and preach with recycled information. Yet what we lack are souls that share their own light from the present. Only one who experiences silence in the now can communicate with another from heart to heart.

I am convinced that human evolution is individual and not collective. Development will not come from organizations but in and through individuals. The human race will take an important step when it transcends the herd and realizes individuality, which is the highest expression of intelligence.

I do not spread my message on a large scale because I do not believe in religion as a social phenomenon. For me, enlightenment belongs to individuals. My books, answers, and talks are not for the collective but for the individual. I express myself as an artist rather than a preacher. Missionaries are interested in your responses to their preaching; they want to win you over to their ideology. If they are successful, you will convert to their "ism"; what matters is the result of their sermon. Like politicians before election day, they only care about winning your vote. They want you to switch from one organization to another and move you into a new prison. On the other hand, true artists are centered and express themselves from within. They are not calculated and do not care if their work receives applause or hisses. They are not worried about praise or criticism. Authentic artists are absorbed in melodies and colors, not in the result of their work.

For my part, I am not interested in your reactions to my words. If they motivate your search for yourself, then continue on your path. In my communication, there is not the faintest intention of convincing anyone of anything. I am not selling an ideology. This is not an attempt to manipulate you or convert you into some "ism." My intention is not to preach but to get closer and to cultivate an intimate relationship with you. For a fraternal relationship, what matters is our private, not public, communication. Any attempt at preaching puts us on the defensive. If I tried to convince you of an ideology, it would ruin our communion, because you would close yourself to my melody.

I simply communicate my vision, and you decide what to do with it. If my song inspires you and you act on it, it is not because of what you have heard, but because of what it has awakened in your heart. Then will you remain complete, whole in yourself. Your decision will not originate from some external ideology or imposed preaching but from your own reality.

The one who needs to leave the cage and fly is you, not your organization, your community, your institution, or your group. You will have to distinguish between illusion and reality yourself, because the realization of what you really are cannot be reached through your religious community, but by sharpening and purifying your own power of discrimination. Your authentic nature will not be given to you by a church, temple, or mosque, but through your own intelligence. Recognizing what is authentic can occur only within an individual. I am obviously not referring to ego-based individualism that society promotes so strongly through religious, political, and moral systems. Such individualism dominates us and impedes our evolution.

I am not addressing my readers, followers, disciples, or even nations or peoples. I am addressing you, the one who is reading these words now. If you are at all able to overcome your conditioning, it will happen within you, because you are the only one who can transcend your ego, through your own powers of discrimination. Only you can cultivate them by observing your mind. Only you can learn to differentiate between darkness and light, day and night, attachment and love. Only you can separate the temporal from the eternal, the real from the apparent, what we are from what we believe we are. Only you will have to die as a personality to be reborn as an individuality.

I have heard you say that you do not consider sex to be an obstacle to spiritual development. On the other hand, there are others who view sex as a hindrance to self-realization. Many paths recommend celibacy or abstinence from sex. Could you clarify your position on sexuality in the spiritual process?

Life is simple, but it becomes complicated when it is grasped through the mind. Thought consists of reactions, memories, conditioning, and so on. The mind belongs to the theoretical dimension, which is made up of thoughts, ideas, concepts, imaginations, and fantasies; thus, it complicates what is simple and sees the world in a very convoluted way. It is not related to the substantial, but to the echo of the essential that is perceived on the surface.

Even though concrete occurrences are reflected in the mind, they do not take place in it. Instead of perceiving a tree, we only perceive our thoughts about the tree. Being in the mind, we do not grasp reality but our ideas and conclusions about it. Instead of living, we think, imagine, dream, idealize, and fantasize about life.

The mind constantly invents difficulties and then seeks to overcome them. However, its remedies only aggravate the disease; solutions cannot be born of the mind, because the mind is the real problem. For example, eating does not hinder spiritual evolution; it simply fulfills certain metabolic needs. It is part of a natural process of acquiring energy. However, thought has turned a natural need into a means of recreation, amusement, and relief, and consequently, into good business. By thinking about food, we have created gastronomy with its restaurants, chefs, and gourmets. This attitude has given rise to eating disorders such as bulimia, anorexia, gluttony, and obesity. After enjoying dinner, we think, "That was so delicious!," and this mental process generates a memory and a desire for repetition. Attraction to pleasure occurs in the mind. Although eating does not delay our evolution, thinking about delicacies and luxurious restaurants gives rise to desires that demand to be satisfied.

Likewise, sleeping, breathing, or having sex are not obstacles to spiritual development. Yet madness begins when these natural needs become part of our mental activity. Thinking, remembering, and fantasizing about sex have led to eroticism, prostitution, and pornography. In our erotic fantasies, we imagine beautiful and perfect beings who never become tired or grow old and always desire us passionately. The dream world has no boundaries, but as reality is limited, not every sexual fantasy can be satisfied. These fantasies doom us to constant dissatisfaction, because it is impossible to find perfect creatures in reality. So in order to resolve the problem of sex, the mind creates methods like celibacy and repression. But just like all of our natural needs, sex is an integral part of life. It is a healthy and natural act, which becomes abnormal only if we experience it through the mind.

Although it is commonly believed that Judeo-Christian tradition rejects sexuality, the Torah does not require celibacy to approach God, nor does it consider it a sign of holiness. The Jewish laws of *taharat ha mishpacha*, or "purity of the family," are not intended to reduce sexual activity, but to prevent it from becoming a mental obsession. The Bhagavad Gita also says that sex is not in conflict with the eternal dharma:

balaṁ balavatāṁ cāhaṁ
kāma-rāga-vivarjitam
dharmāviruddho bhūteṣu
kāmo 'smi bharatarṣabha

I am the strength of the strong, devoid of
passion and desire. I am a sexual life that is
not contrary to religious principles, O lord
of the Bhāratas [Arjuna].

(Bhagavad Gita, 7.11)

As a natural act, sex is not an obstacle on the path
to God. Like any obsession or mental demand, sex
becomes a nuisance in the spiritual process only when
we exaggerate its importance. But if we recognize that
it is a natural phenomenon, it can manifest as love.

Thoughts transform natural needs into objects of
pleasure. When we enjoy, we forget ourselves as egoic
personalities. Thus, food and sex become means to
evade the cause of our suffering and pain, which is
"what we believe ourselves to be." The mind aspires
to repeat moments of pleasure in order to escape from
itself. These reactions give rise to desires that become
obsessive cravings.

When we experience pleasure, we forget the "I" for
a moment. But the ego immediately assumes the role
of the enjoyer and stores the pleasure in memory. In
enlightenment, the "I" is also forgotten, and there is no
longer an egoic personality that feels diminished.

If we are only identified with what is apparent,
our life unfolds on the surface. When we live based
on the mind, superficiality prevails in each and every
way. Those who identify themselves with the physical
body consider the mind to be their inner world. Only
one who has recognized consciousness can notice that

thoughts belong to the surface, and, upon transcending the mind, realize absolute bliss.

Could you explain more about the master-disciple relationship?

Many things in life are not meant to be explained or understood, but to be experienced. Logical analysis will only make us miss the point. It is impossible to understand the master-disciple relationship by listening to others or reading books because it is a mysterious romance... a love story to be lived.

Masters and their disciples do not establish a relationship. What happened between the Baal Shem Tov and his Hassidim, Buddha and his sangha, and Śaṅkara and his *śiṣyas*, was not a relationship but an encounter between darkness and light, between questions and the answer. The disciple is fertile soil; the master, a rain-laden cloud. In this union, duality disappears in the Absolute, the river merges into the sea, the drop vanishes in the ocean, wisdom clears away ignorance, light dissipates darkness, and the human becomes the Divine.

The Sanskrit word *guru* means "one who helps to dissipate darkness":

> *gu-kāras tv andha-kāraś ca*
> *ru-kāras teja ucyate*
> *ajñāna grāsakaṁ brahma*
> *gurur eva na saṁśayaḥ*

It is said that the syllable *gu* is the darkness and that the syllable *ru* is the light. There is no doubt that the guru is, in effect, the supreme knowledge that destroys the darkness of ignorance.

(*Śrī Guru-gītā*, 23)

We find a very similar explanation in the *Vaiṣṇava-kaṇṭha-hāra*:

> *gu-śabdas tv andha-kāraḥ*
> *ru-śabdas tu nirodhakaḥ*
> *andha-kāra-nirodhatvād*
> *gurur ity abhidhyate*

The word *gu* means "darkness" and *ru* means "that which disperses." According to his or her ability to disperse the darkness of ignorance, such a transcendental being is called *guru*.

(*Vaiṣṇava-kaṇṭha-hāra*)

On the dualistic plane, relationships are established between egos: parents and children, sellers and buyers, managers and employees, siblings, lovers, friends, neighbors, and so on. By definition, a relationship needs two. Disciples, in their ignorance, perceive the guru as someone different from themselves; however, from the perspective of the master it is not so. The encounter between the master and the disciple eliminates all separation; everything that disperses and divides fades away, revealing the underlying unity. In this relationship, disciples meet with themselves, because the master is not a somebody but a nobody… an emptiness, a presence, a nothingness.

Arjuna addresses Krishna in the following manner:

sakheti matvā prasabhaṁ yad uktaṁ
he kṛṣṇa he yādava he sakheti
ajānatā mahimānaṁ tavedaṁ
mayā pramādāt praṇayena vāpi

yac cāvahāsārtham asat-kṛto 'si
vihāra-śayyāsana-bhojaneṣu
eko 'tha vāpy acyuta tat-samakṣaṁ
tat kṣāmaye tvām aham aprameyam

Thinking of you as my friend, I have rashly addressed you as "O Krishna," "O Yādava," "O my friend," not knowing your glories. Please forgive whatever I may have done in madness or in love. I have dishonored you many times, jesting as we relaxed, laid on the same bed, sat or ate together, sometimes alone and sometimes in front of many friends. O infallible one, please excuse me for all these offenses.

(Bhagavad Gita, 11.41–42)

Ordinary friendship is often a mutual nourishment of the ego. Most people choose anyone who feeds their self-image as a friend. As Lion Daudi said, "Do you want an advice for success in your relationships? Help others keep up their masks." In general, this is what friendship is all about: helping each other maintain masks. In that sense, masters cannot be considered friends. However, they are the only true friends because they help disciples transcend themselves and go beyond the "I."

Masters acts as enemies of the ego-phenomenon. Their words and actions are like acid for disciples' egos. Gurus' behavior is relentless, devastating, and destructive. Their work consists in eliminating dreams, illusions, and fantasies. Masters are a real disruption aimed at disturbing disciples' sleep.

Society and the media bombard us with offers of comfort, security, and consolation. If you start a company that can offer such benefits, surely your business will be successful. However, closeness to the guru is not for seekers of safety or relief, but only for those who aspire to liberation.

For the disciple, the master is God; for the master, everyone is God. The guru's vision is based on the underlying divine nature of all beings. According to the sacred scriptures, the original guru, or *caitya-guru*, lies in our innermost depths:

> *sarvasya cāham hṛdi sanniviṣṭo*
> *mattaḥ smṛtir jñānam apohanam ca*
> *vedaiś ca sarvair aham eva vedyo*
> *vedānta-kṛd veda-vid eva cāham*

I am seated in everyone's heart, and from me come remembrance, knowledge, and forgetfulness. By all the Vedas, I am to be known. Indeed, I am the compiler of Vedanta, and I am the knower of the Vedas.

(Bhagavad Gita, 15.15)

The *caitya-guru* is the inner spiritual master who resides in the heart and is one with the Self. The two external aspects of the *caitya-guru* are the *dīkṣā-guru* and the *śikṣā-gurus*. The *dīkṣā-guru* eternally guides our soul. *Śikṣā-gurus* instruct us on specific aspects of the spiritual life. Both manifestations are essential, because communication requires external agents, as long as we have not achieved the level needed to connect with the *caitya-guru* directly. If we have the right attitude, we will gradually be able to reconnect with our inner spiritual master.

The presence of the guru inspires and elevates; it is a flower, a sunset, a full moon. Only our identification with the mind separates us from the master. Masters do not offer a path to a distant goal, nor do they teach a theory or doctrine that gives us a specific understanding. Gurus do not preach a particular religion, rather, they *are* their disciples' religion. True disciples do not choose a master within their own religion, but follow the religion through which their gurus choose to express themselves.

People often think that the master-disciple relationship is like the teacher-student relationship. Despite some similarities, there is an enormous difference. Students know that they are searching for information. Disciples, while experiencing a strong urge, do not know the object of their longing; they seek the Truth or God without knowing what these words mean. They aspire to the mystery; they long to lose themselves in the unknown. Students desire to "know about"; disciples want to "be." Students have a clear goal because their impetus is born from the mind, but disciples' motivation knows no words since it emerges from a place prior to the mental plane.

The relationship between a teacher and a student is intellectual in nature; it develops at the mental level. It is a transmission of information intended to give knowledge. The encounter between master and disciples, on the other hand, is existential in nature; it is not about studying or learning but about being. In the scripture *Pirkei Abot*, it is said that Moses received the Torah from Mount Sinai. The master may be a person but could also be a place where our encounter with consciousness happens. This encounter does not happen on the physical or mental plane, but on the spiritual one.

While the student seeks information, the disciple seeks a complete transformation. Disciples have recognized their ignorance and seek to realize their true nature. Teachers teach subjects, while masters teach themselves. True disciples want to learn their masters, who are the essence of the Self.

The teacher imparts knowledge, while the guru is committed to complete epistemological liberation. Pedagogues try to expand the students' storehouse of information, but masters guide us toward a total emancipation from any theory, idea, concept, or conclusion.

When disciples find their master, they have to embark on a transformative process of liberation from the past and the known. Like dust on a mirror, the known prevents us from reflecting reality. Covered by theologies, philosophies, and scriptures, we cannot reflect the Divine. Being part of a certain "ism," we project ideas and concepts upon reality instead of seeing it. The worship of God is replaced by the worship of ideas about God. Idols of stone and bronze do not pose any real danger. True idolatry is to worship mental idols made of thought. Logically, the search for our own ideas cannot lead us to unveil something real. Ideas and words are symbols, but they are not the thing itself. Although symbols can be bridges to the unmanifested plane, there is a danger to remain trapped in them. In order to access Truth, reality, and God, it is imperative to destroy our thought idols and empty ourselves completely of any concept.

The window lets us see the landscape, but the trees and hills do not belong to the window. It is only a hole that lets us see outside. Similarly, the master is a void through which we can glimpse freedom. The guru is not a person but an absence that reveals the mountains. The guru does not allow disciples to attribute the beauty of the landscape to him or her. Disciples often get attached to the individual that they consider their savior or messiah. However, the master will not accept this harmful attitude. Disciples must relate to the master as an open door to the Truth that invites them to step through.

The spiritual master is not only a guide but the path itself, as indicated by *Maitrī Upaniṣad*:

> *uddhartum arhasīty andhodapāna*
> *stho bheka ivāham asmin saṁsāre*
> *bhagavaṁstvaṁ no gatis tvaṁ no gatiḥ*

May you liberate me. In this cycle of repeated births and deaths I am like a frog in a dark well. Your Divine Grace, you are our path, you are our path.

(*Maitrī Upaniṣad*, 1.7)

A very similar concept is presented in the New Testament (John, 14:6): "'I am the way, the Truth, and the Life,' replied Jesus, 'Nobody reaches the Father except through me.'"

Masters fulfill the role of spiritual parents. Just as we receive our physical bodies from our biological parents, through the master we are born in spirit. Our mother is the door to the world, yet the master is the door to the plane of consciousness. However, no one can pass through the gateway in your place, not even the master; only you can cross the threshold.

Democracy might be the most suitable system for modern society, but in certain situations we need to choose other alternatives. An airplane must be flown by a pilot and not based on the democratic vote of the passengers. Doctors should often ignore the preferences of their patients. Likewise, a transformative process cannot be unfolded democratically. Disciples should not expect the work with the master to be democratic, because someone who is sleeping cannot choose whether to wake up or continue sleeping.

A real master is a finger pointing toward freedom; hence, the master will never meet disciples' expectations. Salesmen try to satisfy their clients. Politicians do their best to keep voters happy. Only false masters fulfill the expectations of their followers. Real ones will continuously disillusion them; that is why so few disciples remain with their masters. Real gurus often have "Judahs" and leave behind a trail of disappointed disciples who could not give up their own expectations.

A real disciple will find a real master; a mediocre one will probably surrender to a mediocre master; a false disciple will be drawn to a false master. Nowadays, many people talk about fake masters; however, the fault belongs not just to the gurus, but mostly to the people who are attracted to those who tell them whatever they want to hear.

It is very important for disciples to understand the role of masters. Masters can indicate where the water is, but disciples' thirst will remain unquenched unless they are willing to drink. Although gurus can teach disciples to spread their wings, disciples are the ones who must fly. The master supports and motivates but cannot become self-realized on behalf of the disciple. Just like traffic police, masters can give directions, but it is not their job to bring you to your destination.

The disciple must have an attitude of service and exploration. If you approach a guru, it should be in order to serve and not to be served, to give and not to receive. The guru cannot give you anything that you do not already have. You only need the Self, but you already are the Self; hence, only you can give it to yourself. The guru teaches you the art of giving, so you can give the Self to yourself.

Disciples do not approach a spiritual master in search of knowledge, but when they are weary of information and their hearts have turned into big question marks. They put aside everything they know and become receptive. They ask, examine, and explore, but not through intellectual questioning. The spiritual learning process is not just intellectual but also transcendental.

It is an unconditional encounter where the disciple, thirsty for Truth, asks for nothing. The master, on the other hand, does not promise paradise after death. Disciples do not demand anything because they do not know what they seek. Masters do not promise anything because what they offer is already included in their silence and presence.

The master is a masculine, even when expressed through a female guru. Similarly, even male disciples adopt a female attitude. They approach the master with vulnerability and receptivity. Their attitude is passive and free of defenses. The surrender of every soul in love is feminine in nature. Its openness allows it to be penetrated by the presence of the master.

The cultivation of receptivity and vulnerability prepares us for unconditional surrender, which is an essential step toward total transformation. Surrender comes from the disciple's heart and is never imposed by the master; if it is forced, one should question the veracity of such a guru.

Unconditional surrender is the path toward deep communion between disciple and master. Whoever has not yet found a master can surrender to life, existence, or totality. The important thing is awakening unconditional surrender in one's heart. The disciple does not surrender to someone but to divinity; not to a person but at the feet of Truth. Krishna says in the Bhagavad Gita:

sarva-dharmān parityajya
mām ekaṁ śaraṇaṁ vraja
ahaṁ tvāṁ sarva-pāpebhyo
mokṣayiṣyāmi mā śucaḥ

Abandon all varieties of dharma and simply surrender unto me alone. I shall liberate you from all sinful reactions; do not fear.
(Bhagavad Gita, 18.66)

The evolutionary process that takes place within the master-disciple relationship flourishes from trust, love, and loyalty. The development of the disciple is not the result of a specific activity. The aspirant does not evolve due to a particular practice. Every practice is a preparation, but it does not lead to development itself.

True masters shine but never dazzle. Authentic disciples are on a quest to dissipate darkness; they long to see clearly what is, as it is. Human beings do not perceive the world as it is, but as it appears to them; instead of observing, they project their mental content on what they see. Disciples realize this and seek clarity. The master does not give them anything specific, but only the chance to see what already is. The guru is light and offers clarity to the disciple, who lives in the dark.

oṁ ajñāna timirāndhasya
jñānāñjana-śalākayā
cakṣur unmīlitaṁ yena
tasmai śrī-gurave namaḥ

I was born in the darkest ignorance, and
my spiritual master opened my eyes with
the torch of knowledge. I offer my respectful
obeisances unto him.

(*Śrī Guru-gītā*, 34)

The disciple and the master are both searching.
Disciples seek to open up to unlimited receiving, so that
this wide and unconditional opening allows them to
accept the entire universe. The master, on the other hand,
seeks an appropriate recipient for the infinite secret.

At a superficial glance it would seem that the
disciple gives everything to the guru in exchange for
spiritual elevation. Yet the encounter between the two
is not a give-and-take relationship. The real intention is
to awaken the dormant divine potential that lies in the
disciple. The *Śrī Guru-gītā* says:

yajño vrataṁ tapo dānaṁ
japas tīrthaṁ tathaiva ca
guru-tattvam avijñāya
mūdhāste carate janāḥ

The practice of japa, the rituals of sacrifice,
vows, penance, charity, and pilgrimages

are all a waste of time without a proper understanding of the guru principle.

(*Śrī Guru-gītā*, 24)

All disciples desire to be close to their master. But despite living very near physically, they never manage to feel close to *someone*. The distance they feel is the distance from themselves. The phenomenon of the master is more a presence than a substance, a simultaneous presence and absence. As a presence, the master is completely here and now. As substance, the master is the absence of someone or something objectified in space and time, and lacks the apparent mass and substantiality of the limited egoic phenomenon. The guru is an embodied void... the shadow of the nothingness, a reflection of emptiness on the lake of relativity.

By trying to get closer to where the guru is, we will discover where we actually are. In the presence of the master, disciples recognize themselves. In fact, this is the idea behind the word *satsang*, which means "to sit with the Truth." Satsang is the deep and intimate communion of two presences, two silences emerging as one; what happens between them is a love story, but it is unlike any romance we know. It is not a relationship between two, but a duet of one.

As we contemplate a beautiful piece of art, we might feel embraced by tender peace and refreshing happiness. However, if we analyze the components of the painting in a laboratory, we will not find peace. Happiness does not come from a picture, but from our inner depths. In other words, a colorful canvas connects us to the source of bliss, which always resides within our intimate depths. Similarly, what we experience in the presence of the master is our true nature, or God.

The disciple is a potentiality and the master, a manifestation. The former is a seed; the latter, a tree. The guru represents the possibilities of the disciple; the disciple represents what the guru once was. The master is the disciple's future; the disciple is the master's past. In the presence of the master, disciples are situated in front of their possibilities, before what existence dreams for them.

The spiritual master is the most faithful expression of the Absolute within the relative. The Self expresses itself in the master's silence, glances, and gestures. Before the master, we feel less like a mind or body and more like a being. This presence emanates from the totality of someone who is established in the here and now. To learn from masters, we need to sit close to them and listen to the melody flowing from their soul. In tune with their silence, we will recognize our own peace in the depths of the soul.

Dear Prabhuji, I understand and mostly agree with your criticism of religion. Could you tell me, in your opinion, what is the greatest damage that religion has caused to humanity?

I wish to clarify that I do not criticize religion but institutionalized religion. There is only one true religion, while institutionalized religion has many faces. Because it is social and non-spiritual, there are as many religious "isms" as cultures: "templism," "churchism," "synagogism," and so on.

Religion belongs to the enlightened master, while organized religion belongs to preachers, priests, rabbis, pandits, imams, and the modern "sat-sangists." Authentic religion has flourished in people like Jesus, Buddha, Moses, Muhammad, Śaṅkara, Krishna, Chaitanya, Lao-Tze, or Guru Nanak. Religious "isms" belong to the Pope, the Vatican, the Chief Rabbinate of Israel, and the like.

Jesus did not know about Christianity, Catholicism, or Protestantism. Moses never heard the term *Judaism*. Buddha never imagined that he would become the founder of Buddhism.

I consider myself religious, and hence, my words seem subversive to institutionalized religion. True religion has always reacted against pseudo-spiritual businesses that lease made-up gods and sell us imaginary plots of land for the afterlife, something like a Paradise Real Estate agency. We see this clearly in Jesus's reaction to the merchants at the temple entrance in Jerusalem.

Organized religion is born from fear and the psychological need to find meaning and explanations for life's experiences. It offers an escape from confusion: it explains the incomprehensible and approaches the unattainable. The illusionary and conditioned mind can invent both religious ritualism and symbolism, but it cannot conceive of a sacred god.

Obstructing humanity's access to authentic religion has been the greatest damage institutionalized religion has caused. It has been more interested in preserving the organization than facilitating individual spiritual development. Institutional interests have prevailed over followers' benefits.

All organized religions present themselves as the only true religion. For centuries, they have all tried to deceive humanity by declaring that they own the copyright on the word of God. By insisting that they possessed the Truth, they have contributed to the conditioning of millions of people. By condemning any attempt to question their dogmas, these "isms" have extinguished believers' ability to investigate and examine. They have kept their adherents on the surface by using all kind of ruses such as "doubt is a spiritual weakness," "thinking is pointless," and "investigating is unnecessary."

Throughout history, these "isms" have paralyzed followers' faculty of thought and promoted blind fanaticism. They have convinced them that seeking is futile and have kept them ignorant about themselves. Dogmas have made idiots of the masses. Instead of being axiomatic tools, they have become an end in themselves. Cheap religiosity has for centuries proclaimed to have answers to all questions. It has lacked the humility to accept and revere life's mystery. It does not have enough honesty to publicly admit that not all our questions can be answered. Science has been more honest and accepted that it lacks explanations to some mysteries.

Organized religiosity has impeded any kind of spiritual evolution. One of its strategies has been to disseminate prefabricated arguments. From a young age, it trains and indoctrinates us; it even gives us answers to questions we have not yet formulated. Before we even question the existence of God, it gives us his address, inclinations, desires, and demands.

On the other hand, authentic religion is not exclusive but inclusive: it motivates and supports individuals in their search for Truth. Its aim is to inspire questioning and exploration. It manifests when we transcend the limits of the mind and become free from the conditioning that ensnares us. It is not psychological, as it does not belong to the domain of the mind. It is accessed through observation, not faith, beliefs, or superstitions. It is reached by looking beyond any tradition or custom. What is truly sacred can only happen when fear is overcome, the mind is silenced, and we as egoic phenomena are transcended.

God is not the answer but a clearing of all questions. In Hebrew, the word for *answer* is *tshuva*, or "returning to God." Truth is experienced in the quiet that remains when mental activity ceases. The mystery of existence is revealed when innocent silence is the only answer; that tender silence that answers the question "Do you love me?" A silence that makes everything so obvious that the question fades away. In the Bible, it is described as *kol dmama daka*, or "a voice of delicate silence."

And, behold, the Lord passed by, and a great
and strong wind destroyed the mountains,
and broke in pieces the rocks before the
Lord; but the Lord was not in the wind; and
after the wind an earthquake; but the Lord
was not in the earthquake; and after the
earthquake a fire; but the Lord was not in
the fire; and after the fire a still small voice.

(1 Kings, 19:11–12)

Maybe one of these nights, you will raise your
questions to the sky, and the blinking stars will embrace
you with their deafening and lively silence... Such silent
shouting from the depths of existence will eclipse your
enigmas... Perhaps only then shall you feel a caress of
Truth.

You had a mystical experience at a young age. Then, after 32 years of searching, you became enlightened. I would like to know if your enlightenment was a result of your practices.

At the age of eight, I had a mystical experience. I had the infinite fortune of being initiated by existence. In the silence of the night, the moon and the stars gave me *dīkṣā*. However, a mystical experience is totally different from enlightenment, because you are still present as an observer. Even if you observe the light, whatever is observed is an object, while enlightenment is pure subjectivity.

Enlightenment is always unexpected and accidental. It is not an effect of a cause, nor a result of a practice. No methodology can grant it. Jesus, Buddha, Śaṅkara, Moses, and others awakened to reality under various circumstances. If we examine their lives, we will learn that enlightenment was an accident that happened to them in very particular situations: dancing, singing, walking, sitting quietly, and so on. For some of them, it occurred in the tranquility of their homes; for others, in a mountain cave, in the desert, or the forest. Awakening can surprise you anywhere. Just like falling in love, it is the same experience for all, yet everyone has their own love story.

Spiritual practice, or sadhana, is not meant for the attainment of moksha. The aim of prayer, hatha yoga, *japa*, *prāṇāyāma*, and meditation is not to enlighten us. *Yoga-vidyā* creates appropriate conditions for enlightenment. Its purification methods help overcome obstacles or impediments to facilitate the accident of enlightenment.

We cannot force sleep. In order to fall asleep, we have to create the proper environment: draw the blinds, turn off the light, get into a comfortable bed, relax, and so on. But sleep can only fall upon us of its own accord. Similarly, there is no method for falling in love with someone. All you can do is to create the right conditions. Sleep and love, just like enlightenment, are accidents that simply happen.

Existence is extremely creative and avoids copies. Looking at the ocean waves, the mountains, and the flowers, we notice that life dislikes repetition. Different religions have created methods that mimic the circumstances in which enlightened ones awoke. If the prophet became enlightened while sitting, then the practice is to sit. If the saint found God while dancing, the sadhana is to dance. These activities, however, are not the cause. If one master awoke while sitting, the reason was not the body position or the chair. If another discovered the Divine while dancing, it was not because of the dance.

Before undertaking a practice, it is very important to put it in its place. Every religion has developed its own practices, yet followers have not necessarily achieved the coveted result. Their methods have not always been effective in transcending illusion. Jews, Christians, Hindus, and Buddhists have imitated their prophets for centuries without attaining the desired divine goal. Such practices have transformed religion into a business: whoever pays with the currency of practice will receive the desired merchandise. This has turned us into manipulators and opportunists.

Religion is unveiling our true existence in the reality of the present. If the practice is aimed at some goal, it projects us toward the future. Any sadhana that seeks enlightenment, as elevated as it may be, distracts us from the present moment. The only alternative is to create favorable conditions and cultivate the art of waiting properly; not expecting something in particular but transforming ourselves into unconditional waiting. There is nothing left to do but to meditate with great trust in life. In the right moment, a ray of light will illuminate your soul. In that fatal divine accident, you will perish as "someone" to be reborn as the Whole.

I know that there were
enlightened masters who had
no guru. Could accepting a
master prevent me from following
my own path and hence
postpone my enlightenment?

From the very moment you ask this, you are becoming a disciple. The nature of discipleship is inquiry. Krishna says:

tad viddhi praṇipātena
paripraśnena sevayā
upadekṣyanti te jñānaṁ
jñāninas tattva-darśinaḥ

Try to learn the Truth by approaching a spiritual master. Inquire submissively and render service unto the master. Self-realized souls can impart knowledge unto you because they have seen the Truth.
(Bhagavad Gita, 4.34)

Paripraśnena means "submissive inquiries." Inquiry and service, or *seva*, are the two pillars of the master-disciple relationship.

Many people ask questions, but disciples' inquiries are different. Disciples do not ask out of curiosity, but because these doubts disturb their routine and keep them awake at night; they are vital, a matter of life or death. The quality of the inquiry depends on how intense the quest is. Inquiring is part of a transformative process, because the answers might compel us to make profound changes, to accept uncomfortable situations, or to give up attachments. The guru's responses require commitment and can revolutionize our inner world.

If you want intellectual knowledge about mysticism, spirituality, or religion, studying comparative religions or theology at a university will be enough. A master is only necessary if you are seeking self-realization and are ready to make a greater commitment to the journey. The encounter between disciple and guru is a meeting between questions and the answer. The pedagogue offers answers, but the master *is* the answer.

It is true that over the course of history there have been some enlightened beings who did not need the guidance of a flesh-and-blood master; in fact, it is possible to become enlightened without accepting a master, but not without being a disciple. These virtuosos of spirit had no masters but were great disciples. I call them *virtuosos* because they are an exception to the rule, just like prodigies who compose music at a young age. But if you are not one of them, you will need the help of a master.

If the master were the only obstacle to awakening, everyone who does not have one would be enlightened. If you do not have a guru who hinders you, why are you not yet enlightened? Most people do not accept a spiritual master not because they do not need one, but because they cannot accept being a disciple. Gurus pose a vital danger, because they attack the security of the egoic phenomenon. Obviously, the ego will try to defend itself by saying that it is not necessary, just like a reluctant child on a visit to the dentist.

The master-disciple relationship is eternal; however, it goes through different phases. It resembles our relationship with our biological parents: as children, we depend on their guidance for every last detail, such as when to eat or go to bed, but as we mature, that relationship evolves into something new. Similarly, our spiritual parents may become obstacles for development, but only if they are not transcended in due time.

When we board a train to arrive at a distant city, it is essential to get off when the train arrives at the right station. If we stay seated, we cannot reach our destination. In due course, the master will gladly bless the disciples to go their own way. If they remain attached, the obstacle will not be the guru but the disciples' attitude. Only you can delay or impede your own self-realization.

You often refer to true spiritual seekers. I would like to know who can be considered a spiritual seeker.

Material seekers are motivated by the ambition to satisfy their desires for money, honor, or fame. Dogmatic religious seekers strive to achieve God, paradise, or enlightenment. Someone I consider to be a true spiritual seeker questions everything, including the search and the essence of the searcher.

Material seekers' lives are governed by the yearning to satiate desires for wealth, position, respect, power, and many other things. They spend their lives striving for pleasure, enjoyment, and happiness. This pursuit disconnects them from reality, because their lives revolve around a constant projection of dreams. Their ambitions push them in multiple directions and condemn them to a state of conflict. This inner struggle is also reflected in their relationship with the world and other people. For this reason, spiritual seekers are interested not in satisfying desires but understanding them. They do not attempt to fulfil or repress desires, because even the intention to eliminate them is a desire. Knowing that it is impossible to transcend what one does not understand, they observe and examine their desires.

Spiritual searching begins when we understand that desires bring frustration. We realize that no matter how successful we might become, in the end, our achievements will need to be abandoned. We see that as long as desire is present, we will keep projecting selfish longings upon life. We notice that our ambitions inhibit observation, obstruct access to reality, and prevent us from being in the now. Spiritual inquiry is seeking reality or Truth. Instead of running after the satisfaction of demands and selfish needs, spiritual seekers investigate themselves, their own yearnings, and even the motivations behind their search.

Material seekers dream of achieving whatever is out of reach, whatever they lack. Their search originates from a feeling of deficiency. Spiritual seekers, on the other hand, aspire to recognize what they have; they want to become aware of what already is and perceive it as it is. This is a subtle yet enormous difference. They understand that a superficial life is meaningless, reduced to being born, sleeping, protecting oneself, eating, procreating, and dying. They refuse to see life as a passage from cradle to grave without any kind of evolution. When they become aware of this inconstant reality, they discover that their life is nothing but illusion.

The search can begin only when we face life's miseries. Three walks around the city were enough for Buddha to become aware of the earthly suffering that had been hidden from him behind the closed gates of the palace. It was during these walks that he realized that worldly enjoyment and pleasures were trivial. Having recognized the negative, he began the search for the positive; and it is then that Buddha left the palace in pursuit of real happiness, or absolute bliss.

Throughout history, little has made us more passionate than the search for Truth. From this passion, works like the Bible, the Koran, the Upanishads, the *Zend Avesta*, the *Tao Te Ching*, and the *Dhammapada* were born. Deep theologies and philosophies emerged from these scriptures, but also dogmatic religions, blind beliefs, and fanaticism. Religious seekers wish to experience God or enlightenment; they go through life yearning for lights, opening chakras, and paradises, yet any attempt to satisfy these desires is material. As long as they strive to fulfil their dreams, there will be greed, and they will remain enmeshed in illusion. In the tenacity to satisfy their ambitions, they are like dogs chasing their own tails: the faster they run, the quicker their tails get away. Instead of seeking one's own ideas about God, it is better to aspire for a direct experience. A true spiritual search is existential, not dogmatic.

If our efforts are aimed at attaining God and enlightenment, we will remain with nothing but myths and dogmas in our hands. The search should begin by exploring exactly where we are. If you are a mind, observe and study it. Start by investigating your ego. Question your thoughts instead of condemning them. Get to know your desires instead of suppressing them. Do not ask if God exists; ask if you exist. If you start from the beginning instead of the end, you shall embark on a true evolutionary process of transformation.

When the pursuit of desires is overcome, the spiritual search becomes much simpler. Any difficulty in meditation is a sign that we still have to go beyond the first phase. Only when we are free from desires do we cease to be directed toward the future and situate ourselves in the present. Desires are in the future, while Truth is the now. It is impossible to awaken to reality without overcoming desires. Transcending them means going beyond thought, and that is meditation. Only in the absence of desires does every mental and emotional activity cease, and we can immerse ourselves in the depths of our interior. To situate ourselves in the here and now is to wake up to what is, as it really is. In the present, enlightenment is revealed as a natural consequence.

Enlightenment is not to satisfy a longing, but the inevitable consequence of having gone beyond the mind. The involutive process is not about adding what we lack, but about getting rid of what we have in excess. In fulfilling desires, we achieve, get, acquire, and possess more. Only by undertaking the inner search shall we ease our heavy egoic load.

Ego is a lack of consciousness, while the spiritual search expands consciousness. Instead of struggling to eradicate the ego, we should strive to broaden awareness. Only by looking for ourselves is it possible to get lost, dissolve, and empty ourselves. Transcending the ego is synonymous with full consciousness.

The wave is the individual aspect of the ocean; the ocean is the oceanic aspect of the wave. Examining the components of a drop, we can understand the ocean. Likewise, if we begin by analyzing our individual aspect, we will end up accessing the divine aspect. Inquiring into the personal, we will access the universal. Observing the part, we will understand the Whole. The spiritual quest is just an effort to create the proper situation. When conditions are favorable, we will see that Truth, enlightenment, and God are already there—exactly where we are.

Every time I try to meditate, my mind becomes overactive and scattered: it starts jumping from one idea to another, from one thought to another. Could you give me some advice how to improve my meditation?

According to raja yoga, concentration (*dhāraṇā*) comes before meditation (dhyana). *Dhāraṇā* is the sixth step of the ashtanga yoga of Patañjali, who explains:

deśa-bandhaś cittasya dhāraṇā

Concentration (*dhāraṇā*) is the process of maintaining or fixing the attention of the mind on an object or place.

(*Yoga Sūtra*, 3.1)

Concentration involves willfully and consciously directing the attention at a certain object. Consequently, mental agitation decreases and attention focuses on a single point. Concentration allows us to forget objective reality and facilitates meditation.

Many students, professionals, and artists wish they had better concentration, because it is crucial for their work. Since concentration often does not come easily, we have seen lately the appearance of numerous new methods aimed to improve it. However, without understanding that our mind follows our heart, no technique will help us. It is very difficult to concentrate on something that we do not love. We are truly present wherever our heart is. But we often try to focus on objects that we are not devoted to.

Our interests and cares are not all in one place. Most people have a variety of interests such as basketball, cats, money, children, family, country, and thousands of other things. When looking at them superficially, they appear to be different affections. Yet it is possible to integrate all of them into a single focal point of concentration if we realize the common source hidden behind them.

Life branches out into a large variety of areas, and our activities require integration. For example, work seems to be disconnected from family duties. However, they are deeply intertwined. While working, we actually fulfill our duties as members of a family. The yogic approach integrates our diverse occupations, affections, and inclinations.

Relating to the deity in the proper way may facilitate our integration and concentration. We should understand that the *iṣṭa-devatā*, or "preferred deity," is not an object among many others but includes everything. Therefore, nothing separate from this deity can distract our attention. In our *iṣṭa-devatā*, we can find the same satisfaction that is provided by any attractive object in the universe. If we have a hundred dollars, we also have the cents contained in that sum: we do not lack cents because we only have dollars. By concentrating on the Whole, we will naturally cease to worry about the parts and our mind will stop jumping from one object to another. This concentration spontaneously flows into meditation. Unlike mundane love, devotion to God is inclusive; it contains everything that evokes in us some degree of affection and attraction. Authentic bhakti is born from the understanding that the deity is a representation of the Whole and that the objects disappear to reveal themselves as inseparable parts of God.

The idolatrous attitude is to view God as simply another object among many. A religion limited to the subject-object plane cannot guide us beyond concentration. In order to meditate, we have to stop being religious and forget any ideas, beliefs, or concepts about God. When we transcend duality, we no longer speak of Christianity, Judaism, or Hinduism, but of pure subjectivity.

In meditation, we remove religion in order to enter the realm of pure consciousness, of what is, of the Self. We recognize the ocean in the wave, the Whole in the part, and the Absolute in the depths of our interior. Real concentration leads us to discover that nothing can divert our attention from the one divine nature that underlies everyone and everything.

Dear Prabhuji, what is devotion or bhakti?

Devotion is the purest expression of love; it is love in its absolute purity. Romance happens between people, but devotion is love for existence. In the most intimate depths, all limits that separate us from life evaporate. The boundaries that make us feel like a person separated from the Whole disappear. In this divine love story, any sensation of "me" and "mine" vanishes, and we fuse with life itself.

Devotion is love, not solely physical, mental, or romantic, but spiritual. It is expressed not through the body, mind, or feelings, but arises from the depths of the soul. As we experience devotion, all differences between lover and loved, subject and object, disappear. Krishna says:

> *man-manā bhava mad-bhakto*
> *mad-yājī mām namaskuru*
> *mām evaiṣyasi satyam te*
> *pratijāne priyo 'si me*

Always think of me and become my devotee. Worship me and offer your homage unto me. Thus you will come to me without fail. I promise you this because you are my very dear friend.

(Bhagavad Gita, 18.65)

In a worldly romance, your heart responds to a glance, a touch, or a kiss. In devotion, your heart vibrates with the breeze that caresses the trees, the moon's reflection on a lake, or the perfume of flowers in the air. Your soul dances with the song of birds and the silence of the forest. Wherever you look, you recognize the magic, the mystery, and the divine secret. You hear it in the rustle of the wind, the sound of the waves, and the rumble of river rapids. You feel it in the fragrance of the soil after the rain and in the salty air by the ocean.

Devotion develops gradually from tamasic to rajasic, to sattvic, and finally, to transcendental. Krishna says:

> *karmaṇaḥ sukṛtasyāhuḥ*
> *sāttvikaṁ nirmalaṁ phalam*
> *rajasas tu phalaṁ duḥkham*
> *ajñānaṁ tamasaḥ phalam*

By acting in the mode of goodness (sattva), one becomes purified. Works done in the mode of passion (rajas) result in distress, and actions done in the mode of ignorance (tamas) result in foolishness.

(Bhagavad Gita, 14.16)

Tamasic devotion is mere sentimentalism that creates confusion. Rajasic devotion is passionate and restless and leads to religious fanaticism. Sattvic devotion is peaceful, mature, and serene; its meditative nature encourages introspection. For its part, the devotion that transcends the gunas is a gift of existence that reflects the bliss and clarity of the Self. In the same way, devotees can be tamasic, rajasic, sattvic, or transcendental.

Transcendental devotees are not even interested in liberation: having renounced enlightenment completely, they continually enjoy the nectar of devotion.

Transcendental devotion cannot be reduced to a belief system. It is not born out of a theology but from our innermost depths. It is expressed in different languages and traditions, yet does not belong to any institutionalized religion. Devotion is mentioned in one of the most famous verses of the Bible: *Ve'ahavta et ha'shem elohecha bechol levavchah u'vechol nafshechah u've'chol meodechah*, which means, "And thou shalt love the Lord thy God with all thine heart and with all thy soul, and with all thy might" (Deuteronomy, 6:5). The Koran also tells us: "If you should love Allah , then follow me, [so] Allah will love you and forgive you your sins." (Koran, *Surah Āl 'Imrān*, 31).

Through devotion, we gain access to God. In the Bhagavad Gita, we read:

bhaktyā mām abhijānāti
yāvān yaś cāsmi tattvataḥ
tato māṁ tattvato jñātvā
viśate tad-anantaram

One can understand me as I am only by devotion. And when one is in full consciousness of me by such devotion, he can enter into the Kingdom of God.

(Bhagavad Gita, 18.55)

Love exposes us to the Divine; devotion shows us God. A devotee's heart knows the ultimate Truth of life. It is important to understand the difference between "knowing" and "knowing about." "Knowing about" refers to practiced skills or memorized information: sports, mathematics, languages, and so on. On the other hand, "knowing" expresses a familiarity with someone or something. Knowing God is very different from knowing about anything else in life. For example, your dentist knows about your teeth; your mailman, about your address; your mechanic, about your car. They might recognize your face, but none of them really know you. Similarly, many religious people claim to know God because they know about his address, his language, his desires and inclinations, but you can only know someone you love.

וְהָאָדָם יָדַע אֶת־חַוָּה אִשְׁתּוֹ וַתַּהַר וַתֵּלֶד אֶת־קַיִן וַתֹּאמֶר קָנִיתִי אִישׁ אֶת־יְהֹוָה.

(בראשית, ד', א')

And the man knew Eve his wife, and she conceived and bare Cain, and said, "I have gotten a man from the Lord."

(Genesis, 4:1)

The Bible uses the Hebrew term *yada*, or "knew," to refer to a very intimate relationship.

בְּטֶרֶם אֶצָּרְךָ בַבֶּטֶן יְדַעְתִּיךָ וּבְטֶרֶם תֵּצֵא מֵרֶחֶם הִקְדַּשְׁתִּיךָ נָבִיא לַגּוֹיִם נְתַתִּיךָ.

(ירמיהו א', ה')

Before I formed thee in the belly I knew
you; and before thou camest forth out of
the womb I sanctified thee and I ordained
thee as a prophet unto the nations.

(Jeremiah, 1:5)

Devotees do not *know about* God; rather, they *know* God. Their love allows them to become familiar with Him. Similarly, feelings of respect and surrender help disciples develop an intimate relationship with their spiritual masters, but only devotion will lead to a perfect communion. The devotee is the pinnacle of disciple. Just as those who love know their beloved, only a heart brimming with devotion truly knows God's presence. Their familiarity with the Divine is about wisdom, not information.

Devotion is one of those inexplicable mysteries that transcends logic. Therefore, the nectarous bliss of devotees does not come from what they know about the Lord, but from what they do not know about him. They are like the *gopīs*, who do not know that Krishna is God, but see him as the soul of their lives.

Devotees are indifferent to both suffering and pleasure, to pain and happiness. They eliminate all their preferences, predications, inclinations, and conditioning, as well as any ideas, concepts, or conclusions that might threaten love. As their devotion increases, they diminish as "someone" and disappear, like raindrops of water in the ocean.

Devotion is dying to the apparent and awakening to the real; it is to perish to the ephemeral and be reborn in the true. It is the termination of the personal to make room for the universal; the evaporation of the temporal and the transient to recognize the permanent and the immortal. Devotion is to forget the past and the future in order to observe the fresh dawn of the present. It is to leave behind what was and what should be in order to discover what is. Devotion is to die in time and space and be reborn in the eternal and infinite.

Just as the caterpillar turns into a butterfly, if you love intensely, your love will unfold as devotion. Once your heart is flooded with devotion, you will be moved to worship the stars, the ocean, the trees, and the flowers. Every living being will inspire reverence in you. Your entire life will be transformed into a prayer, and each exhalation into only one hymn: "Thank you." When this divine phenomenon occurs, you become a door to existence, a bridge to the Whole.

To conclude, I would like to share with you what I consider one of the most beautiful devotional masterpieces: *Śikṣāṣṭakam*, the eight verses of Chaitanya:

ceto-darpaṇa-mārjanaṁ bhava-mahā-dāvāgni-nirvāpaṇaṁ
śreyaḥ-kairava-candrikā-vitaraṇaṁ vidyā-vadhū-jīvanam
ānandāmbudhi-vardhanaṁ prati-padaṁ pūrṇāmṛtāsvādanaṁ
sarvātma-snapanaṁ paraṁ vijayate śrī-kṛṣṇa-saṅkīrtanam

> Glory to the Sri Krishna *Saṅkīrtana*, which cleanses the heart of all the dust accumulated for years and extinguishes the fire of conditional life, of repeated birth and death. This *saṅkīrtana* movement is the prime

benediction for humanity at large because it spreads the rays of the benediction moon. It is the life of all transcendental knowledge. It increases the ocean of transcendental bliss, and it enables us to fully taste the nectar for which we are always anxious.

nāmnām akāri bahudhā nija-sarva-śaktis
tatrārpitā niyamitaḥ smaraṇe na kālaḥ
etādṛśī tava kṛpā bhagavan mamāpi
durdaivam īdṛśam ihājani nānurāgaḥ

O my Lord, your holy name alone can render all benediction to living beings, and thus you have hundreds and millions of names like Krishna and Govinda. In these transcendental names you have invested all your transcendental energies. There are not even hard and fast rules for chanting these names. O my Lord, out of kindness you enable us to easily approach you by your holy names, but I am so unfortunate that I have no attraction for them.

tṛṇād api su-nīcena
taror iva sahiṣṇunā
amāninā māna-dena
kīrtanīyaḥ sadā hariḥ

One should chant the holy name of the Lord in a humble state of mind, thinking oneself lower than the straw in the street; one should be more tolerant than a tree, devoid of all sense of false prestige and should be ready to offer all respect to others. In such a state of mind one can chant the holy name of the Lord constantly.

na dhanaṁ na janaṁ na sundarīṁ
kavitāṁ vā jagad-īśa kāmaye
mama janmani janmanīśvare
bhavatād bhaktir ahaitukī tvayi

O almighty Lord, I have no desire to accumulate wealth, nor do I desire beautiful women, nor do I want any number of followers. I only want your causeless devotional service birth after birth.

ayi nanda-tanuja kiṅkaraṁ
patitaṁ māṁ viṣame bhavāmbudhau
kṛpayā tava pāda-paṅkaja-
sthita-dhūlī-sadṛśaṁ vicintaya

O son of Maharaja Nanda [Krishna], I am your eternal servitor, yet somehow or other I have fallen into the ocean of birth and death. Please pick me up from this ocean of death and place me as one of the atoms at your lotus feet.

nayanaṁ galad-aśru-dhārayā
vadanaṁ gadgada-ruddhayā girā
pulakair nicitaṁ vapuḥ kadā
tava nāma-grahaṇe bhaviṣyati

O my Lord, when will my eyes be decorated with tears of love flowing constantly when I chant your holy name? When will my voice choke up, and when will the hairs of my body stand on end at the recitation of your name?

yugāyitaṁ nimeṣeṇa
cakṣuṣā prāvṛṣāyitam
śūnyāyitaṁ jagat sarvaṁ
govinda-viraheṇa me

O Govinda! Feeling your separation, I am considering a moment to be like twelve years or more. Tears are flowing from my eyes like torrents of rain, and I am feeling all vacant in the world in your absence.

āśliṣya vā pāda-ratāṁ pinaṣṭu mām
adarśanān marma-hatāṁ karotu vā
yathā tathā vā vidadhātu lampaṭo
mat-prāṇa-nāthas tu sa eva nāparaḥ

I know no one but Krishna as my Lord, and he shall remain so even if he handles me roughly by his embrace or makes me brokenhearted by not being present before me. He is completely free to do anything and everything, for he is always my worshipful Lord unconditionally.

(*Śrī-caitanya-caritāmṛta,* "*Antya-līlā,*" 20.12, 16, 21, 29, 32, 36, 39, 47)

Dear Prabhuji, according to your teachings, the important thing is to get rid of the mind, but it seems to me that life would be very difficult without the mind. Could you please clarify this?

Residing solely in the mind makes us nonexistent. We live on longings and memories as well as in hopes and dreams about some imaginary future. Instead of perceiving *what is*, we go along in life projecting the illusory on the real. By transcending the mind, we regain the freedom to exist in the reality of the present while coming into harmony with ourselves, with others, and the entire universe.

We are chained to the mind as if it were our master. Transcending the mind means using it rather than being its servants. The mind is useful as long as it does not control our lives. The finite mind should serve the infinite consciousness, not vice versa. Mental slavery leads to suffering and misery, but once we become the masters of our minds, our lives will be divine. My advice is not to get attached to the mind. True mastery is achieved through meditation. The *Dhammapada* states:

> The mind is difficult to subjugate; it is extremely subtle and tends to run after its fantasies. The sage should watch it attentively. A controlled mind leads to real happiness.
>
> The mind by nature is scattered, wondering, and incorporeal. It lives as if hidden in a cave. Those who succeed in overcoming it are liberated from the powerful fetters of illusion.
>
> (*Dhammapada*, 3.4–5)

To overcome the mind does not mean to stop using it, but just to not leave it turned on twenty-four hours a day. Although it is essential to function in the world, it will function more efficiently if we give it some rest. We should use it only when necessary and when not, to forget about it and just *be*. To get rid of the mind is to free ourselves from its dominance and not allow it to control us. We can live with the mind but without identifying with it. Dominated by the mind, we will live in hell, but mastering it, we shall discover ourselves as infinite consciousness.

I use the mind to answer your question, just like I use my feet to walk or my hands to write, but having finished, I rest in the silence of pure consciousness.

What do you mean when you speak of human conditioning?

Our authentic nature is covered up. From an early age, we have been wrapped in names, denominations, definitions, and concepts of who we are. They have dressed us up in endless social conventions, the products of our culture. Such mental covers do not allow us to perceive what we really are. We do not live from our nakedness but dressed in clothes made of what we believe ourselves to be. It was on the banks of the sacred river Yamuna where Krishna hid the clothes of the *gopīs*, his devoted cowgirls, and agreed to give them back only to those who appeared naked before him. Similarly, the spiritual process is about being ready to undress before existence. However, this exposure must be born out of love; it cannot be forced, as in the case of Draupadī, whom the Kurus tried to undress, and who was saved by Krishna as he gave her an endless sari. Lastly, let us remember that significant moment in the life of St. Francis of Assisi when he undressed in front of his parents, the bishop, and the poor.

The egoic phenomenon constantly urges us to hide under our mental clothing. We try to cover our wound called *the ego* and refuse to air it. We want privacy to continue freely satisfying our selfish demands and needs. People often behave differently in public and in private, and very few expose what they really think and feel. We are so covered with clothing that we forget our true nature. Since we hide so well from others, we have a hard time finding ourselves.

In the Book of Genesis, when the first man and the first woman were at their purest, they lived naked, just as they really were.

וַיִּהְיוּ שְׁנֵיהֶם עֲרוּמִים הָאָדָם וְאִשְׁתּוֹ וְלֹא יִתְבֹּשָׁשׁוּ.
(בראשית ב׳, כ״ה)

And they were both naked, the man and his
wife, and were not ashamed.

(Genesis, 2:25)

It was only after the fall that they became aware of
their nakedness and tried to cover themselves; thus, they
were dressed when expelled from paradise.

וַתִּפָּקַחְנָה עֵינֵי שְׁנֵיהֶם וַיֵּדְעוּ כִּי עֵירֻמִּם הֵם וַיִּתְפְּרוּ עֲלֵה תְאֵנָה
וַיַּעֲשׂוּ לָהֶם חֲגֹרֹת.
(בראשית ג׳, ז׳)

And the eyes of them both were opened,
and they knew that they were naked; and
they sewed fig leaves together, and made
themselves aprons.

(Genesis, 3:7)

Masters live in utter nakedness. Like an open book,
they do not hide anything from anyone. In 1 Samuel,
we see that prophesying is related to nudity:

וַיִּפְשַׁט גַּם־הוּא בְּגָדָיו וַיִּתְנַבֵּא גַם־הוּא לִפְנֵי שְׁמוּאֵל וַיִּפֹּל עָרֹם
כָּל־הַיּוֹם הַהוּא וְכָל־הַלָּיְלָה עַל־כֵּן יֹאמְרוּ הֲגַם שָׁאוּל בַּנְּבִיאִם.
(שמואל א׳, י״ט, כ״ד)

And he stripped off his clothes also, and prophesied before Samuel in like manner, and lay down naked all that day and all that night. Wherefore they say, "Is Saul also among the prophets?"

(I Samuel, 19:24)

We are born without any clothing. Then, pure consciousness becomes covered by ideas, thoughts, concepts, and conclusions. Human conditioning is made of social garments that hide consciousness. To meditate is to observe our garments—physical, mental, emotional, and energetic—and gradually strip of ourselves. The retroprogressive process is to undress consciousness. Enlightenment is simply to be, abide in our authenticity, and live stripped of all clothes.

Dear Prabhuji, what can we do to become enlightened?

The book of Genesis begins like this:

"(1) In the beginning God created the heaven, and the earth. (2) And the earth was without form, and void; and darkness was upon the face of the deep. And the spirit of God moved upon the face of the waters. (3) And God *said, Let there be light*: and there was light. (4) And God saw the light, that it was good; and God *divided* the light from the darkness. (5) And God called the light Day, and the darkness he called Night. And the evening and the morning were the first day. (6) And God said, Let there be a firmament in the midst of the waters, and let it *divide* the waters from the waters. (7) And God *made* the firmament, and divided the waters which were under the firmament from the waters which were above the firmament: and it was so. (8) And God called the firmament Heaven. And the evening and the morning were the second day. (9) And God said, Let the waters under the heaven *be gathered* together unto one place, and let the dry land appear: and it was so. (10) And God called the dry land Earth; and the gathering together of the waters called he Seas: and God saw that it was good. (11) And God said, Let the earth *bring forth* grass, the herb yielding seed, and the fruit tree yielding fruit after his kind, whose seed is in itself upon the earth: and it was so. (12) And the earth brought forth grass, and herb yielding seed after his kind, and the tree yielding fruit, whose seed was in itself, after his kind: and God saw that it was good. (13) And the evening and the morning were the third day. (14) And God said, Let there be lights in the firmament of the heaven to *divide* the day from the night; and let them be for signs, and for seasons, and for days, and years: (15) And let them be for lights in the firmament of the heaven to give light upon the earth: and it was so. (16) And God *made* two great lights; the greater light to rule the day, and the lesser light to rule the night: he made the stars also. (17) And God set them in the firmament of the heaven to give light upon the earth. (18) And to rule over the day and over the night, and to *divide* the light from the darkness: and God saw that it was good. (19) And the evening and the morning were the fourth day. (20) And God said, Let the waters *bring forth* abundantly the moving creature that hath life, and fowl that may fly above the earth in the open firmament of heaven. (21) And God *created* great whales, and every living creature that moveth which the waters brought forth abundantly, after their kind, and every winged fowl after his kind: and God saw that it was good. (22) And God blessed them, saying, Be fruitful, and multiply, and fill the waters in the seas, and let fowl multiply in the earth. (23) And the evening and the morning were the fifth day. (24) And God said, Let the earth *bring forth* the living creature after his kind, cattle, and creeping thing, and beast of the earth after his kind: and it was so. (25) And God made the beast of the earth after his kind and cattle after their kind, and every thing that creepeth upon the earth after his kind: and God saw that it was good."

(Genesis, 1:1–25)

The light of the first day is different from the light emitted by the luminaries created on the fourth day. If we pay attention to the text, we will see that God does not create or produce light but only says: "Let there *be* light," and there was light. During the process of creation, on the other hand, God performs different actions: He *divided* the light from the darkness; He *divided* the waters from the waters; He *created* great whales and every living creature, and so on. However, God did not perform any action related to the first light; rather, it appeared after a divine expression that reflected His desire.

According to Rabbi Sa'adiah ben Joseph Gaon, verse 3 refers to the light of divine glory, and the fact that God *said* indicates that God *wanted*. When God desires light, He does not need to make it, but just to mention it.

In verse 2, it is said, "And the earth was without form, and void; and darkness was upon the face of the deep…" The darkness is only upon the face, on the outside. The light lies in the depths of the interior. It is not necessary to create it, but only to aspire to it, and it will become manifested.

God creates. However, He did not make the light of the first day: He only mentioned it. If the light were a divine creation, it would be impossible for us to create it, because human beings can only destroy, compose, and arrange, but not create. In verse 3, the Bible bestows on us the power to aspire to clarity. It tells us that when we long for light, it will manifest from the depths of darkness. Although we lack the ability to create from nothing, we can desire light and illuminate the darkness.

King David says:

עוּרָה כְבוֹדִי עוּרָה הַנֵּבֶל וְכִנּוֹר אָעִירָה שָּׁחַר.
(תהלים נ"ז, ט')

Awake, O my soul! Awake, O harp and lyre!
I will wake the dawn.

(Psalms, 57:8)

Basing on this verse, Rabbi Joseph Karo opens the *Shulchan Aruch* as follows:

יתגבר כארי לעמוד בבוקר לעבודת בוראו, שיהא הוא
מעורר השחה.
(שולחן ערוך,אורח חיים, סעיף א')

Let one be strong like a lion to get up in the
morning for the sake of serving his creator,
to wake, or illuminate, the dawn.
                    (*Shulchan Aruch*, *Orach Haim*, verse 1)

The *Shulchan Aruch* begins like the Torah: rising in
the morning to continue the very work of the creator,
to wake up or illuminate the dawn, which means to
illuminate the morning. That is, human beings can
awaken the dawn, and if they want light… there will be
light! Later on, Rabbi Joseph Karo offers instructions
for how to perform this divine work: by keeping God
in front of oneself… always.

שִׁוִּיתִי יְהֹוָה לְנֶגְדִּי תָמִיד.

(תהילים טז', ח')

I have set the Lord before me constantly.
                    (Psalms, 16:8)

If you really aspire to clarity, you have only to
desire it. You just need to follow your soul's thirst for
the light.

When Jesus spoke again to the people, he
said, "I am the light of the world. Whoever
follows me will never walk in darkness, but
will have the light of life."
                    (New Testament, John 8:12)

How can I control the mind or at least pacify it?

This is a frequent question because many people seek to alleviate the anxiety caused by constant mental activity. After a hard day at work, they wish to find peace at home, but mental activity does not cease. They yearn for their yearly vacation, but the mental bustle does not stop even then. Even while sleeping, the noise continues as dreams or nightmares.

Patañjali says this in his scripture *Yoga Sūtra*, *yogaś citta-vṛtti-nirodhaḥ*, or "yoga occurs when all mental activity ceases." The mind is not a solid object but an activity; therefore, it is possible to dissolve it. It is like a dance: when the movement stops, the dance simply disappears. Similarly, the mind is movement. The speed of thoughts makes the mind appear solid, just as fan blades look like a solid circle because they rotate at a high speed.

If we look at a crowd from a distance, we cannot recognize individuals. But when we get closer, the mass fades away, and individuals are revealed. In the same way, if we look closely at the mind, we see thoughts in motion like waves in the ocean. As we observe mental content, we cease identifying with the thoughts and perceiving them as "ours." Attentive observation of mental activity reveals our true nature as consciousness.

Thoughts are verbal reactions to what is perceived. Because experiences are temporary, our memory tries to retain the sensations they evoke. Thus, it verbalizes what happens to us in order to perpetuate itself and communicate emotions. At a certain point, verbalization replaces experience itself, just like tourists who are too busy taking photos to enjoy the view. As a child, I used to go on vacation with my uncle, who liked to photograph everything. It always seemed to me that he could enjoy the sea and the trees solely through his little machine. While everyone else was enjoying the trip, he wanted nothing but to take photos. I felt that he was exchanging sensations for a collection of pictures. He often only remembered places and experiences after looking at his photo albums. Just like a camera can block the landscape, the mind can obstruct experience. It is more important to stop verbalizing our feelings than to dominate the mind. Such verbalization is one of the main obstacles for meditation.

Generally, we only stop verbalizing in extreme circumstances. In dangerous situations, thinking loses importance, and we experience life directly. Those who are attracted to extreme sports search for moments when their lives depend on every tiny reaction. Their thoughts are silenced, and they experience the moment firsthand. When we downplay the importance of the present experience, words manifest. While verbalizing, we stop experiencing and start interacting with life from our memory: we live the present based on our past. Staying in the present moment, or reality, requires mental silence.

Since the mind does not really exist, it is impossible to dominate it. Nor is there anyone beyond the mind who can control it. Whoever boasts of mastering the mind has not transcended it but has succeeded in having one part—the ego—control the rest. The ultimate reality is observation. Through observation, the mind is not mastered but disappears. From consciousness, we realize that all mental and emotional activity, like clouds crossing the sky, are only passing occurrences. In fact, we are not limited by the mind itself, but when we get identified with its content. When this identification ceases, our mental or emotional activity cannot limit us.

Whoever manages to escape from the mental prison has nothing to pacify. Instead of being the ruler of your mind, I humbly advise you to be its observer. To transcend the mind, you must settle into consciousness and from there, observe everything that is observable. Being the source of all virtue, observation allows us to transcend impurity. From the very moment that you observe, you are situated in your authenticity.

Get rid of everything that you see until only observation remains, which, obviously, cannot be removed because there is nothing and no one that can discard it. Any effort to silence or dominate the mind is a superficial activity. Remember that all spiritual development happens from the inside out, and never the other way round. To observe or to meditate is to situate ourselves in our original nature. Through meditation, you will recognize yourself as an infinite and silent space.

וְהִסְתַּכֵּל בִּשְׁלשָׁה דְבָרִים וְאִי אַתָּה בָא לִידֵי עֲבֵרָה- דַּע מַה
לְמַעְלָה מִמְּךָ:
עַיִן רוֹאָה
וְאֹזֶן שׁוֹמַעַת,
וְכָל מַעֲשֶׂיךָ בַּסֵּפֶר נִכְתָּבִין.

(פרקי אבות ב׳, א׳)

> Reflect on three things and you will never come to sin; know what is above you: an eye that sees, an ear that hears, and all your deeds are written in a book.
>
> (*Pirkei Avot*, 2.1)

Reality is not a story limited to space and time. To experience it, we must transcend the body and mind; it is consciousness that transcends birth and death. Our true nature is meditation, and when the presence of consciousness is recognized, we cease to identify with the mind and the objective reality of the body. We disappear as something or someone and are reborn as ultimate reality.

Dear Prabhuji, we see that enlightened masters have been very different from each other. Could you explain how they retain their personality and share the teachings in such different ways?

Your question presupposes that differences between people originate in the ego and that those who transcend it should be similar. Nothing is further from the truth: the realization of our authentic nature as nothingness dissolves the "I" but not individuality.

The more self-centered we are, the more we resemble the rest of humanity. The ego is mass-produced; it lacks originality. It reacts to different situations following the same acquired patterns of behavior. Only when we dissolve into the transcendental can our singularity be expressed.

The ego is an illusion or appearance: the more we cling to it, the more we become disconnected from existence. As we transcend it, we die as a false entity, but our existence does not cease. When we stop living from the limited "I," we become rooted in our true self.

Personality is a bundle of repetitive and automatic reactions; it is a collection of masks that we choose for different situations, different disguises for every occasion. We acquire them by imitating our parents, family, neighbors, friends, teachers, managers, favorite singers, and preachers. Our personality is just the role that we play in society's stage; it is an imitation, an expression of our conditioning, and a manifestation of what we have acquired throughout life. It is only a superficial appearance that covers our authenticity. When the "I am" dissolves, an eternal "beingness" emerges. This quality of *being* is vital, pure, fresh, and immaculate. The darkness of our personality disappears in the light of our individuality.

It is impossible to manifest our individuality without first overcoming conditioning. Individuality does not come from society but from the depths of consciousness itself. As the name implies, it is indivisible and integral. It manifests as an expression of our intrinsic nature when the ego is transcended. In order to access individuality, self-knowledge is absolutely necessary. Those who have ceased to live from the experience of the ego can be unique and original.

The awakening of our individuality is the height of self-realization. Enlightened beings express themselves in their own way and have their peculiar style; they play an original melody and display their unique colors. Although they connect to the same essence, they express it in a unique way. They all realize the one reality but share the experience with incomparable originality. Never again will another Buddha, Jesus, Krishna, Śaṅkara, or Baal Shem Tov walk this planet. We will never see anyone like them again, because their individuality was original, incomparable, and unrepeatable.

While it is true that egos can manifest certain dissimilarities, even in their differences, they are very much alike. On the other hand, the differences between enlightened beings are essential and unprecedented. We find a real dissimilarity between Chaitanya dancing in the streets and Buddha sitting in silence; between a flutist like Krishna and a leader like Moses. Beings that have achieved unity have no similarities and are incomparable.

One who transcends and dissolves in the emptiness simply *is*. But this *being* is extremely singular, unique, unlike anybody else who ever was or will be. What dissolves or evaporates is the ego; what is real remains and expresses itself as individuality.

Enlightened beings share a common denominator: Truth. At the same time, each message has its own style and presents a unique path that leads to eternity.

The paths to infinity are diverse; thus, it is futile to look for similarities. Although they lead to the same Truth, they are totally different. If you try to find similarities between the Torah and the Bhagavad Gita, or between the Koran and the Upanishads, you will conclude that one of them is false.

Just as many colors form a beautiful painting, many spiritual paths create a wonderful harmony, and it is in this harmony where they all meet. If we hear musical notes without the rest of the symphony, we will not enjoy the melody. If we focus on a single color, we will be unable to appreciate the painting. But if we dare to observe the harmony expressed by all the individualities, we will perceive the Truth.

There are those who revere you as an enlightened spiritual master, yet I have often heard you vehemently reject this label. Could you explain why it causes you so much discomfort to be considered a guru?

Throughout history, human beings have worshiped saints and prophets; they have placed them on a pedestal, claiming that awakening is not within reach of ordinary people. Those who would consider me an "enlightened master" will think it is impossible for them to achieve the heights of consciousness that I describe; they will erroneously attribute special abilities to me that they believe they lack. But in fact, I am an ordinary, simple, and common human. Like everybody else, I have had successes and made mistakes in my life. I am just a curious being who investigates life and himself, one who lives in the adventure of exploring existence and questions everything.

Besides that, I am simply afraid of losing friends. If you consider me a person like any other, conversation and interchange are possible. We can undertake the adventure of investigating and exploring existence together; we can meet for coffee to talk about the subjects that we are passionate about and evaluate the paths that the giants of the spirit have laid out for us. But as soon as you think I am enlightened, you accept my words without question, and there is no longer any room for inquiry or friendship. I become the one who knows, and you become the ignoramus submerged in darkness. From the moment you wear a rosary with my picture, our dialogues become monologues, my opinions are absolute and irrefutable, and my talks are considered lessons. It will be the end of the get-together. You will just repeat my words without thinking. But it is not my intention to do as professional preachers and religious promoters have done for generations. My job is simply to inspire others in their own search.

"There are those who revere you as an enlightened spiritual master."

I am not a guru, but I cannot forbid others to consider themselves my disciples. Just as I decide whether to be a master or not, others can also choose to be disciples if they wish. I do not have the right to approve or reject the opinions of others about my humble self. Everyone has the freedom to think what they want and reach their own conclusions. There are those who consider me an enlightened master, while others think I am a charlatan. Although I respect both opinions, they are, in fact, no concern of mine. Please consider me a simple "guy" who is focused on putting words together and painting them. I prefer to be counted among artists—a musician who composes melodies and shares what happens to him with whoever is interested.

I would like to know why my mind resists meditating.

It is not surprising that your mind resists, because meditation is like the mind's suicide. If you still think, it is a sign that meditation has not happened yet.

The mind is always active, because its essence is dynamism. It is not a solid object but an activity. Like a dance, the mind is movement, and if it stops, it disappears. Do not search for techniques or methods to pacify the mind, because as long as there is a mind, there can be no peace. Peace is the disappearance of the mind. In fact, the mind is nothing more than a contraction in consciousness; it has no real existence.

You say that the mind resists. Yet thoughts are not an obstacle for meditation, because you only need to observe your mental activity. When we observe without intervening, time vanishes, and we notice that even if the mind stops, we do not cease to exist. We believe we are the mind, and we have completely forgotten our reality. Therefore, we do not live according to what we really are but to what we believe ourselves to be.

Unlike the brain, the mind is not a product of nature. The brain is organic, while the mind is mechanical. The brain is an integral part of our physiology; the mind is a creation of society—a product of family, tradition, customs, institutionalized religion, and ideologies. Society shapes our mind and thus dominates us. Our mind is controlled both by politicians and organized religion. Transcending it means freeing ourselves from a foreign domination over our lives. One who has overcome the mind uses the brain and thinks free of conditioning.

When we meditate, mental activity decreases and, in turn, fear is born. Since we believe ourselves to be the mind, we experience a fear of death. Patañjali mentions the fear of death, or *abhiniveśāh*, as one of the five human afflictions that gives rise to all other fears. To meditate is to know ourselves as emptiness. The experience of nothingness awakens us to the reality of our immortality. When the mind evaporates, the only thing that dissipates is conditioning, the legacy of innumerable generations. It is our mental conditioning that resists meditation; our false identification refuses to die. But when we transcend the mind, a reunion with life and with ourselves awaits us. Then we become fully conscious and absolutely blissful.

How can I improve my
relationships with others?

If we look at how we relate to each other and the world around us, several questions may arise: Why are there so many murderers, wars, and acts of terror? Why are we destroying the environment? Why aren't we capable of establishing sincere relationships with our family and friends? Why is it so hard for us to relate to others without creating conflicts, controversies, and tension?

Human relations are sets of interactions between individuals created through communication, which are necessary in our lives. These relationships make up what we call *society*.

The chaos that reigns in the world today has its origins in human conditioning, which is the source of all sorrow, confusion, contradiction, conflict, misery, and suffering. As a consequence, humanity is fractured in different nations, languages, cultures, ideologies, religions, and so on.

This conflict and discord in society is due to the disorderly way we relate to one another, which is, in turn, a reflection of our internal disorganization. In order to attain harmony, it is necessary to develop self-discipline. Not the discipline that comes from repression, but the discipline that is born from understanding ourselves and our relationships with others.

Understanding how we relate to others can be very helpful in understanding ourselves, because our relationships reflect us like mirrors.

Delving deeper into our relationships, we discover that we create images of ourselves and others. These mental images become our own reference points. We replace information about our anatomy and physiology with a mental image of our physical appearance. The self-image is an individual vision that we have of ourselves, a mental self-portrait that includes a collection of characteristics, abilities, talents, attitudes, appearance, virtues, defects, and so on. All these qualities—whether real or imaginary—form the image that we believe we are, and constitute our identity.

By internalizing and storing others' judgments of us, we draw a mental sketch of ourselves. We build up that self-image based on the opinions of others and our interpretations of them. Ultimately, this mental image is a diagram made up of opinions that we have recorded.

Similarly, we create images of others based on our self-image. Since we are the reference point, we see others the same way we perceive ourselves. Because we conceive of ourselves as an image, we also conceive of others—even of God and the Truth—as images. The set of images begins and ends in us. In fact, we remain idolaters as long as we live our lives based on this self-image.

Our self-image is formed by ideas and opinions of others we have acquired when interacting with them. The main contributors have been our parents, but our relatives, teachers, partners, friends, and acquaintances have also done their part.

From a very young age, our loved ones have contributed to the formation of an image we identify with. Our behavior was shaped through reactions of approval and disapproval: they made it very clear for us what we had to do to gain their appreciation by being good boys and girls. Do you not remember your parents' phrases? "This is not the José Luis I know!" However, this "José Luis" was not *me* but an image, a role that I played in order to satisfy them.

Based on these opinions, we create either a positive or negative image of ourselves. Throughout life, we continue to accumulate perceptions and evaluate ourselves. Thus, according to the circumstances, we choose a role—a writer, athlete, musician, politician, businessman, husband, son, uncle, and so forth—and we identify with it.

Since the image is made up of others' opinions, it does not contain anything real; it is made up of speculations, hypotheses, deductions, presumptions, suppositions, fictions, illusions, and expectations. Our image is disconnected from the world of facts.

That self-image affects us mentally, emotionally, physically, and socially. Based on that image, we choose our friends, clothing, jobs, careers, gestures, vocabulary, and places to visit.

Depending on our needs, we opt to be doctors, musicians, dancers, sinners, or even religious people. Our triumphs cause us to create images of winners, and our failures, of losers. Thus, we respond to life based on who we believe we are and not who we really are.

The image consists of stored sensory perceptions we receive from the world around us. Since sense perceptions are dynamic, the image continuously evolves. For this reason, although the image mostly forms in the childhood and adolescence, it continues developing throughout our lives.

Why do we create images? The mind creates images because it is incapable of knowing, categorizing, and completely defining a human being. The human being is a mystery, and this enigma threatens the mind and makes it feel out of control when it cannot objectify and, hence, possess something. The images protect us from our insecurity and create an illusory sense of safety. Without them, it would be like living the first day at school or a new job every day. We run away from the danger of moving into the unknown in order to experience the feeling of security and the control of "knowing" others.

Thus, the image is an escape from pain and suffering. For example, lonely people create an image that allows them to receive as much attention as possible. Motivated by this need for human warmth, they develop an image of an artist or public speaker. Their inferiority complex leads them to develop a self-image of superiority that helps them escape from suffering.

We also create images of others: we know someone— be it our wife, our son, or a colleague—and we go on accumulating their words, intonations, movements, attitudes, reactions, and moments that we have shared with them, whether annoying or enjoyable. With time, we create an image of that person made of this collection of memorized perceptions.

Human relationships are, in fact, links between images: people relate to others based on self-images and address others' images that they have created. In this way, being true idolaters, we perceive neither ourselves nor others.

It is impossible to cultivate and develop true relationships between images. If we form our images out of clothes, actions, and words, it is impossible to truly relate with one another. Ideas and conclusions about our fellow beings prevent us from knowing who they really are.

Therefore, as long as our relationships are based on images, they will not be true. Only when all representations drop, we will discover ourselves, and know who others are.

Even personal pronouns—you, he, or she—are only piles of memories. For example, when I feel affection for someone, I actually become attached to a series of incidents and situations recorded in my mind. Do I really know the person I say "I love you" to? Whom do I reject when I say "I can't stand you"? Do I even know to whom I refer with the word "I" that I use so much? The mental function of registering and recording is indispensable for survival; however, it is an obstacle when relating to one another.

As a consequence, humanity is divided and fractured. How can a Jew really know a Muslim while maintaining the prejudice that all Arabs are bloodthirsty terrorists who cause pain and suffering to innocent victims? How can an Arab see a Jew as he or she is, while thinking that all Jews are criminals? Only when we eradicate the images that we have created of others will we attain true peace and put an end to racism and xenophobia.

We make up images in search of refuge, but they end up restricting our own freedom. As time goes by, we can only act according to the images we have created. In this life, everything that gives us a sense of security at first ends up limiting us.

As the years go by, we feel ourselves closed in and suffocated inside the thick walls of the image we have built in order to feel protected. Security limits us, and the more secure we wish to be, the more isolated and disconnected from life we become.

In order to protect our image, we create a powerful defense system and reject or ignore anything that can damage it. Eventually, we do not live according to what we are, but according to what we believe we are. If we are watchful whether we are offended or glorified, we will remain indifferent to both insult and flattery. What we call *moksha*, or "liberation," is to be liberated from this image, and self-inquiry, or *ātma-vicāra*, is not to seek a certain image but to discover "who I am."

The problem is not thinking but making up images through thinking. The image is "the thinker" who is sustained through memory. Since all images are based on the past, they obstruct us from seeing the reality and trap us in an illusory world of memories and fantasies. As long as we live based on images, we remain disconnected from the present, reality, and the world of facts.

In order to establish real relationships, we must destroy the images we have of ourselves and others, which means our self-destruction as individuals. That annihilation must also put an end to the mechanism that nourishes the image, otherwise, it won't be long before a new image emerges. The process of elimination consists in observing the phenomenon with alert attention. If we are able to perceive the world without recording it and memorizing it, we can move through life without creating representations of ourselves or others.

We make up mental images due to lack of attention. Our relationships should be based on watchfulness in the present rather than mental recordings of the past. Thought itself is a result of memory, experience, limited knowledge, and lack of attention. When we concentrate, mental activity decreases. When we are conscious, we do not create images.

Many approach a master because the image they have created of themselves is in harmony with an ashram, yoga, the clothes, the art, the incense, the Sanskrit names, and so on. As a rule, such people quickly elaborate an image of the guru.

However, very few of us approach a master longing to see and seeking the help of someone who can point out those painful internal wounds that we have tried to ignore. Masters will not nourish the image or satisfy its desires; quite the contrary, they will bring attention to those painful places of the past and invite us to watch.

If we surrender to a master but foster a hidden agenda of nourishing our image, being in the guru's presence will be unbearable, and eventually, we will leave. On the other hand, if we want to really see, surely we will be blessed with the grace of observation.

Psychology offers valuable instruments to improve our self-esteem and reinforce our own image. Therapists can help us find a better way to conceptualize ourselves and place us on the path to normative functioning in society. However, the master's work is to lead us to the supernormal, to transcend the image, to go beyond, and totally liberate us from it. Creating and maintaining our image makes us susceptible to injury and offense, whereas living without it allows us to experience freedom and peace.

Living without images means experiencing the world without recording, accumulating, or storing our experiences; it means observing reality without memorizing our perceptions.

If we wish to observe a tree, any thought, interpretation or idea about the tree will prevent us from observing it directly. Living without images means living meditatively and watching without reacting or memorizing.

Clear perception of reality requires complete internal silence and total freedom from all thoughts. The superimposition of our memory on observations takes away clarity. We cannot watch through the filter of our memories of situations, moments, discussions, offenses, and so forth. Attention means looking without trying to alter what we see.

Being present, completely attentive, and watchful of this moment's reality means that the image we have made up about ourselves will disappear. Our death as images occurs when situating ourselves in the present. In the Bhagavad Gita, Krishna says:

> *na tvevāham jātu nāsam*
> *na tvam neme janādhipāḥ*
> *na caiva na bhaviṣyāmaḥ*
> *sarve vayam ataḥ param*

There was never a time in which I, or you,
or all of these kings did not exist. And in the
future, none of us will cease to exist.

(Bhagavad Gita, 2.12)

Krishna refers both to his own individual existence and that of others in the past and future, without mentioning the present. What we are now is not definable. The here and now are the acid that melts all images.

When we talk about the present moment, we think it is a unit of time related to the past and future. However, if we think about it more carefully, we will see that what we call *now* is not really clear to us.

We perceive the now as the transition from the past to the future. But how can we define the present itself without relating it to yesterday and tomorrow?

For example, if we take the present as a unit of time, we can refer to the current year. If it is March, then January and February are past, despite being within the current year, and the upcoming months are in the future. Therefore, a shorter period of time is needed in order to define the present.

Let us take the current month. But within the current month, some days belong to the past and others to the future. Then, let us take a day. If we refer to a day as the present time unit, we will see that the same thing happens with hours. Then, let us take an hour, but the same happens with minutes. If we take a minute as the present, we will see that it comprises some seconds in the past and others in the future. The same thing occurs with a second, and so on: we enter into an infinite regression.

We can call a time unit *pure past* or *pure future*. For instance, last year belongs wholly to the past; next year, to the future. But what can we call *pure present*? Any unit we choose as present can be divided. It seems that there is no such unit of time that is completely devoid of past or future and may be called *now*.

If we seek the present as a time unit devoid of past and future, we will reach a dimensionless unit of time. A "now" that could be subdivided into past and future would not be "pure present." That is, the present time is a time that cannot be subdivided.

We may think that nothing can exist without time. However, within the indivisible moment we find the one consciousness that transcends time and space. The present is awareness and being completely aware implies situating ourselves in the now.

Attention is only possible in the present. We cannot be attentive to the past or future, because they are made of memories and imaginations, which lack consciousness. When we reach the indivisible unit, we will rest in consciousness. The essential nature of the present is awareness. To live in the present is to be aware.

Just as with the now, the place that we call *here* can be divided infinitely: both are dimensionless. In the same way that searching for the "now" shows us that the present is not a unit of time, searching for the "here" makes us aware that every "there" is illusory. For example, when we move an empty jar, it seems that the space contained inside it moves too. But the inner space is not different from the outer one. That emptiness within the jar is its oceanic aspect, which we all have. Within our physical, mental, and emotional periphery, we have a "here" that constitutes the center of our existence. The "here" and the "now" are other terms for referring to consciousness.

Since we live deeply rooted in the past, the image that we have made up is stale. Although we move in the present, we do so based on the past, on "what was." The reality is the present, but if we live as images, we are memory. We only see the past and future and think that the now is an imaginary point between yesterday and tomorrow. The past seems real to us because it resides in our memory, and the future, in our hopes. Nonetheless, it is impossible to trap the reality of the present. Unlike the past that we store in our memory and the future that we hold in our imagination, the present slips between our fingers and can be neither possessed nor held. When we wish to perceive the now, it is still future, and when we think we have trapped it, it is already past. When we aspire to experience the now, it belongs to the future, and when we notice that we have experienced it, it is already in the past. The image is thought, and therefore, it is time. Our reality, on the other hand, is attention and awareness. The image does not know the now, because the present is consciousness.

For an ordinary person, the present is illusory, and only the past and future are real. But for an enlightened being, the now is all there is. Along with the realization of our true nature, the past and the future lose their reality, and the present becomes real.

We live in and through the image we have created of ourselves. That image is memory, a bundle of recollections. It is a corpse made of what we wanted to do and never did; it contains our frustrations, past ambitions, and unfulfilled dreams. The image is dead, and therefore, it does not allow us to touch life. It distances us from reality and isolates us from existence.

Since the image is composed of the past, it clings to, retains, and imprisons the known. Protecting the past, the image actually protects itself. The future is nothing but a projection of times gone by, a yesterday with some small modifications. Life is unpredictable, but our image escapes to the past and wants to repeat it.

Bound by the image, we react according to behavioral patterns. In certain situations, we become irritated or offended. However, it is not *us* who reacts. These expressions arise from our memory. We believe we are the origin of our actions, so we try to rationalize them. In these attempts, we blame others for our anger, tension, and sadness. In fact, we do not react because of anybody else; rather, it is only an excuse to rationalize our behavior.

In spiritual maturity, we no longer blame others for our emotions and behavior. Searching for excuses is the wrong direction and will keep us on the surface. If we looked inward instead of running after those we think are guilty of our misery, rage, bitterness, or anger, we will be able to find the origin of our pain.

Our reactions stem from the past, from the image we have created. If we focus our attention on the past, we will become aware of the causes of our suffering. These wounds can be healed if we observe them attentively, as they are mere products of unconsciousness, illusions, and dreams.

We react from the dark corners of our unconscious. When we observe these corners, awareness acts like a healing power. In fact, the only thing that can liberate us from the past is awareness: observing our unconsciousness until we liberate ourselves from the captivity of the past. Living based on the image we have created means letting the past live instead of us; it means accepting the yoke of the old. Only if we liberate ourselves from the past's captivity will we be able to discover the present. Our self-image is only a trunk filled with the past and future, storing what happened before and what hasn't happened yet. As long as we continue to live hidden behind masks, it is impossible to get closer to the present.

When you experience sorrow, pain, jealousy, violence or depression, look inward. As you penetrate your image, you go back in time. Do not do anything; only observe attentively, without reacting. If you judge, you will not be able to observe, because these feelings run to the unconscious when they are condemned. If your image feels accused, it will hide again. Assume the position of a witness and merely observe compassionately without interfering.

Evaporating the image can only happen when we situate ourselves in the present and perceive reality, free from reactions and interpretations.

Meditation means watching ourselves in silence. For this, no action is required, since any effort comes from our image of being "doers." Situating ourselves in the present moment and watching requires deep internal alchemy. Choosing to observe the world instead of reacting to it is the great change: the transformation from "doer" to "witness." To meditate is to contemplate ourselves without objectivizing ourselves while experiencing the presence of what we really are, here and now.

Can you help me understand the
Buddhist concept of emptiness?

Emptiness or *śūnyatā* (*suññatā* in Pali) is one of the fundamental topics in Buddhism. The West understands emptiness as absence, or a lack of something. On the other hand, the East sees it as presence, or the existence of space and silence.

When we visualize a room, we think of its structure—walls, doors, windows, and ceiling—but not of its interior space, without which the room is uninhabitable. Similarly, when we look at a painting, we pay attention to the shapes but not to the emptiness of the background, although its absence would make the shapes indiscernible.

Imagine a kitchen knife made of a wooden handle and a sharp steel blade. With use, the handle breaks, and we replace it. After a few years, the blade wears down, and we buy a new one. Although we have replaced each of its parts, we still think of the knife as the same object. But would you say that it is the original knife? Furthermore, does that knife really exist, or is it just a mental concept? A few years ago, the handle was part of a tree, which, in its turn, had been only a seed, nourished by water and nutrients. Neither the blade existed; it was metal buried in the depths of the earth. Both elements have a temporal existence and constantly change.

Variety belongs solely to the superficial realm. There are differences between a glass, a cup, a bucket, and a pot, but not between their interior spaces. Nor does the inner emptiness differ from the outer emptiness. When a bottle breaks, we can see that the two are not different. With the bottle shattered, the illusion of the difference between inside and outside disappears.

Emptiness does not refer to a mere lack of matter but to the absence of an entity independent of every other object or phenomenon. According to this, objects and entities exist only because the mind defines them as such.

A person seems to us a uniform unit. However, a body is nothing more than an interaction of cells, organs, bones, and flesh made of substances that constantly change. It is not the same as it was yesterday or will be tomorrow. Likewise, the mind is a continuous flow of ideas and feelings that unceasingly change. In fact, this "someone" exists only in the outer wrapping, in the clothing.

Although we constantly change, we believe we have the same identity throughout our lives; however, it is impossible for us to identify exactly what we call "I" because this egoistic concept belongs to the surface. Our inner reality is not solid but just a presence. We are born, live, and disappear in the infinite space of consciousness. Just as the movement of the waves does not affect the depths of the sea, our actions, words, and thoughts do not influence our imperturbable emptiness. All dynamism occurs on the surface—that is, at a physical, mental, and emotional level. Our actions, whether mundane or spiritual, neither degrade nor purify the inner emptiness. A sacred action decorates the outer walls of a building; a profane one stains them. However, both decorations and stains remain on the exterior, while the interior is undisturbed. This absolute emptiness, where everything happens, remains untouchable.

In the course of our lives, the word "I" is undoubtedly the one we use the most. In classical thinking, "I" corresponds to the soul or the subject who speaks, but nobody has yet managed to locate it. In fact, there is no such thing as an autonomous "I"; we are part of an omnipresent infinite "I". The egoic phenomenon consists in considering ourselves a separate entity. However, our existence is not independent in any way: physically, we depend on water, air, food, and sleep. Our life depends on that of our ancestors as well as flowers, trees, stars, and the planet. When we think we are separate entities, we limit and minimize ourselves.

The problem stems from the way we have been programmed to perceive the world around us. Our senses divide reality into subject and object. We perceive that things have certain substantiality. But if we look for an independent "I," we will only find emptiness. The people we know are concepts or ideas that we label as "someone." This concept is very difficult to overcome while we conceive the world solely from a dualistic perspective. Enlightenment means moving in the world without an ego—being integral parts of totality.

Buddhism denies solidity and substantiality but not the existence of the universe and the Self. By pouring water from a bottle, you fill it with emptiness. Emptiness is not synonymous with non-existence or absence; rather, it implies fullness. If we empty ourselves of hatred, we will be filled with peace. If we empty ourselves of words, we will be filled with silence. True peace manifests itself with the discovery that the "I" does not exist. Once the egoic phenomenon is transcended, there is nothing left to defend or promote, and absolute emptiness is experienced. Every effort to achieve is futile. Having overcome the contradiction between everything and nothing, we will awaken to our original nature. By emptying ourselves, we will overflow with plenitude.

Prabhuji

H.H. Avadhūta Śrī Bhaktivedānta Yogācārya
Ramakrishnananda Bābājī Mahārāja

About Prabhuji

Prabhuji is a writer, painter, an *avadhūta*, the creator of Retroprogressive Yoga, and a realized spiritual master. In 2011, he chose to retire from society and lead the life of a hermit. Since then, his days have been spent in solitude, praying, writing, painting, and meditating in silence and contemplation.

Prabhuji is the sole disciple of H.D.G. Avadhūta Śrī Brahmānanda Bābājī Mahārāja, who in turn is one of the closest and most intimate disciples of H.D.G. Avadhūta Śrī Mastarāma Bābājī Mahārāja.

Prabhuji was appointed as the successor of the lineage by his master, who conferred upon him the responsibility of continuing the sacred *paramparā* of *avadhūtas*, officially appointing him as guru and ordering him to serve as Ācārya successor under the name H.H. Avadhūta Śrī Bhaktivedānta Yogācārya Ramakrishnananda Bābājī Mahārāja.

Prabhuji is also a disciple of H.D.G. Bhakti-kavi Atulānanda Ācārya Mahārāja, who is a direct disciple of H.D.G. A.C. Bhaktivedānta Swami Prabhupāda.

Prabhuji's Hinduism is so broad, universal, and pluralistic that at times, while living up to his title of *avadhūta*, his lively and fresh teachings transcend the boundaries of all philosophies and religions, even his own. His teachings promote critical thinking and lead us to question statements that are usually accepted as true. They do not defend absolute truths but invite us to evaluate and question our own convictions. The essence of his syncretic vision, Retroprogressive Yoga, is self-awareness and the recognition of consciousness. For him, awakening at the level of consciousness, or the transcendence of the egoic phenomenon, is the next step in humanity's evolution.

Prabhuji was born on March 21, 1958, in Santiago, the capital of the Republic of Chile. When he was eight years old, he had a mystical experience that motivated his search for the Truth, or the Ultimate Reality. This transformed his life into an authentic inner and outer pilgrimage. He has completely devoted his life to deepening the early transformative experience that marked the beginning of his process of retroevolution. He has dedicated more than fifty years to the exploration and practice of different religions, philosophies, paths of liberation, and spiritual disciplines. He has absorbed the teachings of great yogis, pastors, rabbis, monks, gurus, philosophers, sages, and saints whom he personally visited during years of searching. He has lived in many places and traveled the world thirsting for Truth.

From an early age, Prabhuji noticed that the educational system prevented him from devoting himself to what was really important: learning about himself. Despite his parents' insistence, he stopped attending conventional school at the age of 11 and engaged in autodidactic formation. Over time, he would become a serious critic of the current educational system.

Prabhuji is a recognized authority on Eastern wisdom. He is known for his erudition in the *Vaidika* and *Tāntrika* aspects of Hinduism and all branches of yoga (*jñāna, karma, bhakti, haṭha, rāja, kuṇḍalinī, tantra, mantra,* and others). He has an inclusive attitude toward all religions and is intimately familiar with Judaism, Christianity, Buddhism, Sufism, Taoism, Sikhism, Jainism, Shintoism, Bahaism, and the Mapuche religion, among others. He learned about the Druze religion directly from the scholars Salach Abbas and Kamil Shchadi.

Prabhuji studied Christian theology in depth with H.H. Monsignor Iván Larraín Eyzaguirre at the Veracruz Church in Santiago de Chile and with Mr. Héctor Muñoz, who holds a degree in theology from the Universidad Católica de la Santísima Concepción.

His curiosity for Western thought led him to venture into the field of philosophy in all its different branches. He specialized in Transcendental Phenomenology and the Phenomenology of Religion. He had the privilege of studying intensively for several years with his uncle Jorge Balazs, philosopher, researcher, writer, and author of *The Golden Deer.* He studied privately with Dr. Jonathan Ramos for a few years, a renowned philosopher, historian, and university professor graduated from the Catholic University of Salta, Argentina. He also studied with Dr. Alejandro Cavallazzi Sánchez, who holds an undergraduate degree in philosophy from the Universidad Panamericana, a master's degree in philosophy from the Universidad Iberoamericana, and a doctorate in philosophy from the Universidad Nacional Autónoma de México (UNAM).

Prabhuji holds a doctorate in Vaishnava philosophy from the respected Jiva Institute in Vrindavana, India, and a doctorate in yogic philosophy from the Yoga Samskrutum University.

His profound studies, his masters' blessings, his research into the sacred scriptures, and his vast teaching experience have earned him international recognition in the field of religion and spirituality.

His spiritual search led him to study with masters of diverse traditions and travel far from his native Chile to places as distant as Israel, India, and the USA. Prabhuji studied Hebrew and Sanskrit to deepen his understanding of the holy scriptures. He also studied Pali at the Oxford Centre for Buddhist Studies. Furthermore, he learned ancient Latin and Greek from Javier Álvarez, who holds a degree in Classical Philology from the Sevilla University.

His father, Yosef Har-Zion ZT"L, grew up under strict discipline because he was the son of a senior police sergeant. As a reaction to this upbringing, Yosef decided to raise his own children with complete freedom and unconditional love. Prabhuji grew up without any pressure. During his early years, his father showed his son the same love regardless of his successes or failures at school. When Prabhuji decided to drop out of school to devote himself to his inner quest, his family accepted his decision with deep respect. From the time his son was ten years old, Yosef talked to him about Hebrew spirituality and Western philosophy. They engaged in conversations about philosophy and religion for days on end and late into the night. Yosef supported him in whatever he wanted to do in his life and his search for Truth. Prabhuji was the authentic project of freedom and unconditional love of his father.

At an early age and on his own initiative, Prabhuji began to practice karate and study philosophy and religion. During his adolescence, no one interfered with his decisions. At the age of 15, he established a deep, intimate, and long friendship with the famous Uruguayan writer and poet Blanca Luz Brum, who was his neighbor on Merced Street in Santiago de Chile. He traveled throughout Chile in search of wise and interesting people to learn from. In southern Chile, he met machis who taught him about the rich Mapuche spirituality and shamanism.

Two great masters contributed to Prabhuji's retroprogressive process. In 1976, he met his first guru, H.D.G Bhakti-kavi Atulānanda Ācārya Swami, whom he would call Gurudeva. In those days, Gurudeva was a young *brahmacārī* who held the position of president of the ISKCON temple at Eyzaguirre 2404, Puente Alto, Santiago, Chile. Years later, he gave Prabhuji first initiation, Brahminical initiation, and, finally, he initiated Prabhuji into the sacred order of renunciation called *sannyāsa* within the Brahma Gaudīya Sampradāya. Gurudeva connected him to the devotion to Krṣṇa. He imparted to him the wisdom of bhakti yoga and instructed him in the practice of the *mahā-mantra* and the study of the holy scriptures.

In 1996, Prabhuji met his second guru, H.D.G. Avadhūta Śrī Brahmānanda Bābājī Mahārāja, in Rishikesh, India. Guru Mahārāja, as Prabhuji called him, revealed that his own master, H.D.G. Avadhūta Śrī Mastarāma Bābājī Mahārāja, had told him years before he died that a person would come from the West and request to be his disciple. He commanded him to accept only that particular seeker. When he asked how he would identify this person, Mastarāma Bābājī replied, "You will recognize him by his eyes. You must accept him because he will be the continuation of the lineage."

From his first meeting with young Prabhuji, Guru Mahārāja recognized him and officially initiated him into the *māhā-mantra*. For Prabhuji, this initiation marked the beginning of the most intense and mature stage of his retroprogressive process. Under the guidance of Guru Mahārāja, he studied Advaita Vedanta and deepened his meditation.

Guru Mahārāja guided Prabhuji on his first steps toward the sacred level of *avadhūta*. In March 2011, H.D.G. Avadhūta Śrī Brahmānanda Bābājī Mahārāja ordered Prabhuji, on behalf of his own master, to accept the responsibility of continuing the lineage of *avadhūtas*. With this title, Prabhuji is the official representative of the line of this discipolic succession for the present generation. Besides his *dikṣā-gurus*, Prabhuji studied with important spiritual and religious personalities, such as H.H. Swami Dayananda Sarasvatī, H.H. Swami Viṣṇu Devānanda Sarasvatī, H.H. Swami Jyotirmayānanda Sarasvatī, H.H. Swami Pratyagbodhānanda, H.H. Swami Swahananda of the Ramakrishna Mission, and H.H. Swami Viditātmānanda of the Arsha Vidya Gurukulam. The wisdom of tantra was awakened in Prabhuji by H.G. Mātājī Rīnā Śarmā in India.

Prabhuji wanted to confirm his *sannyāsa* initiation in an Advaita Vedanta lineage. His *sannyāsa-dīkṣā* was confirmed by H.H. Swami Jyotirmayānanda Sarasvatī, founder of the Yoga Research Foundation and disciple of H.H. Swami Śivānanda Sarasvatī of Rishikesh.

In 1984, he learned and began to practice Maharishi Mahesh Yogi's Transcendental Meditation technique. In 1988, he took the *kriyā-yoga* course on Paramahaṁsa Yogananda. After two years, he was officially initiated into the technique of *kriyā-yoga* by the Self-Realization Fellowship.

In Vrindavana, studied the bhakti yoga path in depth with H.H. Narahari Dāsa Bābājī Mahārāja, disciple of H.H. Nityananda Dāsa Bābājī Mahārāja of Vraja.

He also studied bhakti yoga with various disciples of His Divine Grace A.C. Bhaktivedānta Swami Prabhupāda: H.H. Kapīndra Swami, H.H. Paramadvaiti Mahārāja, H.H. Jagajīvana Dāsa, H.H. Tamāla Kṛṣṇa Gosvāmī, H.H. Bhagavān Dāsa Mahārāja, and H.H. Kīrtanānanda Swami, among others.

Prabhuji has been honored with various titles and diplomas by many leaders of prestigious religious and spiritual institutions in India. He was given the honorable title *Kṛṣṇa Bhakta* by H.H. Swami Viṣṇu Devānanda (the only title of Bhakti Yoga given by Swami Viṣṇu), disciple of H.H. Swami Śivānanda Sarasvatī and the founder of the Sivananda Organization. He was given the title *Bhaktivedānta* by H.H. B.A. Paramadvaiti Mahārāja, the founder of Vrinda. He was given the title *Yogācārya* by H.H. Swami Viṣṇu Devānanda, the Paramanand Institute of Yoga Sciences and Research of Indore, India, the International Yoga Federation, the Indian Association of Yoga, and the Shri Shankarananda Yogashram of Mysore, India. He received the respectable title *Śrī Śrī Rādhā Śyam Sunder Pāda-Padma Bhakta Śiromaṇi* directly from H.H. Satyanārāyaṇa Dāsa Bābājī Mahant of the Chatu Vaiṣṇava Saṁpradāya.

Prabhuji spent more than forty years studying hatha yoga with prestigious masters in classical and traditional yoga, such as H.H. Bapuji, H.H. Swami Viṣṇu Devānanda Sarasvatī, H.H. Swami Jyotirmayānanda Sarasvatī, H.H. Swami Satchidananda Sarasvatī, H.H. Swami Vignanananda Sarasvatī, and Śrī Madana-mohana.

He attended several systematic hatha yoga teacher training courses at prestigious institutions until he achieved the level of Master Ācārya. He has completed studies at the following institutions: the Sivananda Yoga Vedanta, the Ananda Ashram, the Yoga Research Foundation, the Integral Yoga Academy, the Patanjala Yoga Kendra, the Ma Yoga Shakti International Mission, the Prana Yoga Organization, the Rishikesh Yoga Peeth, the Swami Sivananda Yoga Research Center, and the Swami Sivananda Yogasana Research Center.

Prabhuji is a member of the Indian Association of Yoga, Yoga Alliance ERYT 500 and YACEP, the International Association of Yoga Therapists, and the International Yoga Federation. In 2014, the International Yoga Federation honored him with the position of Honorary Member of the World Yoga Council.

His interest in the complex anatomy of the human body led him to study chiropractic at the prestigious

Institute of Health of the Back and Extremities in Tel Aviv, Israel. In 1993, he received a diploma from Dr. Sheinerman, the founder and director of the institute. Later, he earned a massage therapy diploma at the Academy of Western Galilee. The knowledge he acquired in this field deepened his understanding of hatha yoga and contributed to the creation of his own method.

Retroprogressive Hatha Yoga is the result of Prabhuji's efforts to improve his practice and teaching methods. It is a system based especially on the teachings of his gurus and the sacred scriptures. Prabhuji has systematized various traditional yoga techniques to create a methodology suitable for Western audiences. Retroprogressive Yoga aims to experience our true nature. It promotes balance, health, and flexibility through proper diet, cleansing techniques, preparations (*āyojanas*), sequences (*vinyāsas*), postures (*asanas*), breathing exercises (*prāṇayama*), relaxation (*śavāsana*), meditation (*dhyāna*), and exercises with locks (*bandhas*) and seals (*mudras*) to direct and empower *prāṇa*.

Since his childhood and throughout his life, Prabhuji has been an enthusiastic admirer, student, and practitioner of classic karate-do. From the age of 13, he studied different styles in Chile, such as kenpo and kung-fu, but specialized in the most traditional Japanese style of shotokan. He received the rank of black belt (third dan) from Shihan Kenneth Funakoshi (ninth dan). He also learned from Sensei Takahashi (seventh dan) and practiced Shorin Ryu style with Sensei Enrique Daniel Welcher (seventh dan), who granted him the rank of black belt (second dan). Through karate-do, he delved into Buddhism and gained additional knowledge about the physics of motion. Prabhuji is a member of Funakoshi's Shotokan Karate Association.

Prabhuji grew up in an artistic environment and his love of painting began to develop in his childhood. His father, the renowned Chilean painter Yosef Har-Zion ZT"L, motivated him to devote himself to art. He learned with the famous Chilean painter Marcelo Cuevas. Prabhuji's abstract paintings reflect the depths of the spirit.

Since he was a young boy, Prabhuji has been especially drawn to postal stamps, postcards, mailboxes, postal transportation systems, and all mail-related activities. He has taken every opportunity to visit post offices in different cities and countries. He has delved into the study of philately, the field of collecting, sorting, and studying postage stamps. This passion led him to become a professional philatelist, a stamp distributor authorized by the American Philatelic Society, and a member of the following societies: the Royal Philatelic Society London, the Royal Philatelic Society of Victoria, the United States Stamp Society, the Great Britain Philatelic Society, the American Philatelic Society, the Society of Israel Philatelists, the Society for Hungarian Philately, the National Philatelic Society UK, the Fort Orange Stamp Club, the American Stamp Dealers Association, the US Philatelic Classics Society, Filabras – Associação dos Filatelistas Brasileiros, and the Collectors Club of NYC.

Based on his extensive knowledge of philately, theology, and Eastern philosophy, Prabhuji created

"Meditative Philately" or "Philatelic Yoga," a spiritual practice that uses philately as the basis for practicing attention, concentration, observation, and meditation. Meditative Philately is inspired by the ancient Hindu *maṇḍala* meditation and it can lead the practitioner to elevated states of consciousness, deep relaxation, and concentration that fosters the recognition of consciousness. Prabhuji wrote his thesis on this new type of yoga, "Meditative Philately," attracting the interest of the Indian academic community due to its innovative way of connecting meditation with different hobbies and activities. For this thesis, he was honored with a PhD in Yogic Philosophy from Yoga-Samskrutum University.

Prabhuji lived in Israel for many years, where he furthered his studies of Judaism. One of his main teachers and sources of inspiration was Rabbi Shalom Dov Lifshitz ZT"L, whom he met in 1997. This great saint guided him for several years on the intricate paths of the Torah and Chassidism. The two developed a very intimate relationship. Prabhuji studied the Talmud with Rabbi Raphael Rapaport Shlit"a (Ponovich), Chassidism with Rabbi Israel Lifshitz Shlit"a, and the Torah with Rabbi Daniel Sandler Shlit"a. Prabhuji is a great devotee of Rabbi Mordechai Eliyahu ZT"L, who personally blessed him.

Prabhuji visited the United States in 2000 and during his stay in New York, he realized that it was the most appropriate place to found a religious organization. He was particularly attracted by the pluralism and respectful attitude of American society toward freedom of religion. He was impressed by the deep respect of both the public and the government for religious minorities. After consulting his masters and requesting their blessings, Prabhuji relocated to the United States. In 2003, the Prabhuji Mission was born, a Hindu church aimed at preserving Prabhuji's universal and pluralistic vision of Hinduism and his Retroprogressive Yoga.

Although he did not seek to attract followers, for 15 years (1995–2010), Prabhuji considered the requests of a few people who approached him asking to become his monastic disciples. Those who chose to see Prabhuji as their spiritual master voluntarily accepted vows of poverty and life-long dedication to spiritual practice (*sadhāna*), religious devotion (*bhakti*), and selfless service (*seva*). Although Prabhuji no longer accepts new disciples, he continues to guide the small group of monastic disciples of the Ramakrishnananda Monastic Order that he founded.

In 2011, Prabhuji founded the Avadhutashram (monastery) in the Catskills Mountains in upstate New York, USA. The Avadhutashram is the headquarters of the Prabhuji Mission, his hermitage, and the residence of the monastic disciples of the Ramakrishnananda Monastic Order. The ashram organizes humanitarian projects such as the Prabhuji Food Distribution Program and the Prabhuji Toy Distribution Program. Prabhuji operates various humanitarian projects, inspired in his experience that serving the part is serving the Whole.In January 2012, Prabhuji's health forced him to officially renounce managing the mission. Since then, he has lived in solitude, completely away from the public, writing and absorbed in contemplation. His message does not promote collective spirituality, but individual inner search.

Prabhuji has delegated the choice to his disciples between keeping his teachings exclusively within the monastic order or spreading his message for the public benefit. Upon the explicit request of his disciples, Prabhuji has agreed to have his books published and his lectures disseminated, as long as this does not compromise his privacy and his life as a hermit.

In 2022, Prabhuji founded the Institute of Retroprogressive Yoga. Here, his most senior disciples can systematically share Prabhuji's teachings and message through video conferences. The institute offers support and help for a deeper understanding of Prabhuji's teachings.

Prabhuji is a respected member of the American Philosophical Association, the American Association of Philosophy Teachers, the American Association of University Professors, the Southwestern Philosophical Society, the Authors Guild, the National Writers Union, PEN America, the International Writers Association, the National Association of Independent Writers and Editors, the National Writers Association, the Alliance Independent Authors, and the Independent Book Publishers Association.

Prabhuji's vast literary contribution includes books in Spanish, English, and Hebrew, for example, *Kundalini Yoga: The Power is in you*, *What is, as it is*, *Bhakti-Yoga: The Path of Love*, *Tantra: Liberation in the World*, *Experimenting with the Truth*, *Advaita Vedanta: Be the Self,* commentaries on the *Īśāvāsya Upanishad* and the *Diamond Sūtra*.

About the Prabhuji Mission

Prabhuji, H.H. Avadhūta Śrī Bhaktivedānta Yogācārya Ramakrishnananda Bābājī Mahārāja, founded the Prabhuji Mission in 2003, a Hindu church aimed at preserving his universal and pluralistic vision of Hinduism.

The main purpose of the mission is to preserve Prabhuji's teachings of Pūrvavyāpi-pragatiśīlaḥ Yoga, or Retroprogressive Yoga, which advocates for a global awakening of consciousness as the radical solution to humanity's problems.

The Prabhuji Mission operates a Hindu temple called Śrī Śrī Radha-Śyāmasundara Mandir, which offers worship and religious ceremonies to parishioners. The extensive library of the Retroprogressive Yoga Institute provides its teachers with abundant study materials to research the various theologies and philosophies explored by Prabhuji in his books and lectures. The Avadhutashram monastery educates monastic disciples on various aspects of Prabhuji's approach to Hinduism and offers them the opportunity to express devotion to God through devotional service by selflessly contributing their skills and training to the Mission's programs, such as the Prabhuji Food Distribution program, a weekly event in which dozens of families in need from Upstate New York receive fresh and nutritious food.

Service and glorification of the guru are fundamental spiritual principles in Hinduism. The Prabhuji Mission, as a traditional Hindu church, practices the millenary *guru-bhakti* tradition of reverence to the master. Some disciples and friends of the Prabhuji Mission, on their own initiative, help to preserve Prabhuji's legacy and his interfaith teachings for future generations by disseminating his books, videos of his internal talks, and websites.

ABOUT THE AVADHUTASHRAM

The Avadhutashram (monastery) was founded by Prabhuji in the Catskills Mountains in upstate New York, USA. It is the headquarters of the Prabhuji Mission and the hermitage of H.H. Avadhūta Śrī Bhaktivedānta Yogācārya Ramakrishnananda Bābājī Mahārāja and his monastic disciples of the Ramakrishnananda Monastic Order.

The ideals of the Avadhutashram are love and selfless service, based on the universal vision that God is in everything and everyone. Its mission is to distribute spiritual books and organize humanitarian projects such as the Prabhuji Food Distribution Program and the Prabhuji Toy Distribution Program.

The Avadhutashram is not commercial and operates without soliciting donations. Its activities are funded by Prabhuji's Gifts, a non-profit company founded by Prabhuji, which sells esoteric items from different traditions that Prabhuji himself has used for spiritual practices during his evolutionary process. Its mission is to preserve and disseminate traditional religious, mystical, and ancestral crafts.

Avadhutashram
Round Top, NY, USA

THE RETROPROGRESSIVE PATH

The Retroprogressive Path does not require you to be part of a group or a member of an organization, institution, society, congregation, club, or exclusive community. Living in a temple, monastery, or *āśram* is not mandatory, because it is not about a change of residence, but of consciousness. It does not urge you to believe, but to doubt. It does not demand you to accept something, but to explore, investigate, examine, inquire, and question everything. It does not suggest being what you should be but being what you really are.

The Retroprogressive Path supports freedom of expression but not proselytizing. This route does not promise answers to our questions but induces us to question our answers. It does not promise to be what we are not or to attain what we have not already achieved. It is a retro-evolutionary path of self-discovery that leads us from what we think we are to what we really are. It is not the only way, nor the best, the simplest, or the most direct. It is an involutionary process par excellence that shows what is obvious and undeniable but usually goes unnoticed: that which is simple, innocent, and natural. It is a path that begins and ends in you.

The Retroprogressive Path is a continuous revelation that expands eternally. It delves into consciousness from an ontological perspective, transcending all religion and spiritual paths. It is the discovery of diversity as a unique and inclusive reality. It is the encounter of consciousness with itself, aware of itself and its own reality. In fact, this path is a simple invitation to dance in the now, to love the present moment, and to celebrate our authenticity. It is an unconditional proposal to stop living as a victim of circumstance and to live as a passionate adventurer. It is a call to return to the place we have never left, without offering us anything we do not already possess or teaching us anything we do not already know. It is a call for an inner revolution and to enter the fire of life that only consumes dreams, illusions, and fantasies but does not touch what we are. It does not help us reach our desired goal, but instead prepares us for the unexpected miracle.

This path was nurtured over a lifetime dedicated to the search for Truth. It is a grateful offering to existence for what I have received. But remember, do not look for me. Look for yourself. It is not me you need, because you are the only one who really matters. This life is just a wonderful parenthesis in eternity to know and love. What you yearn for lies in you, here and now, as what you really are.

Your unconditional well-wisher,
Prabhuji

PRABHUJI TODAY

Prabhuji is retired from public life

Prabhuji is the sole disciple of H.D.G. Avadhūta Śrī Brahmānanda Bābājī Mahārāja, who is himself one of the closest and most intimate disciples of H.D.G. Avadhūta Śrī Mastarāma Bābājī Mahārāja.

Prabhuji was appointed as the successor of the lineage by his master, who conferred upon him the responsibility of continuing the sacred *paramparā* of *avadhūtas*, officially appointing him as guru and ordering him to serve as Ācārya successor under the name H.H. Avadhūta Śrī Bhaktivedānta Yogācārya Ramakrishnananda Bābājī Mahārāja.

Prabhuji is also a disciple of H.D.G. Bhakti-kavi Atulānanda Ācārya Mahārāja, who is a direct disciple of H.D.G. A.C. Bhaktivedānta Swami Prabhupāda.

In 2011, he chose to retire from society and lead the life of a hermit. Since then, his days have been spent in solitude, praying, writing, painting, and meditating in silence and contemplation. He no longer participates in *sat-saṅgs*, lectures, gatherings, meetings, retreats, seminars, study groups, or courses. We ask everyone to respect his privacy and do not try to contact him by any means for gatherings, meetings, interviews, blessings, *śaktipāta*, initiations, or personal visits.

Prabhuji's teachings

As an *avadhūta* and a realized spiritual master, Prabhuji has always appreciated the essence and spiritual wisdom of a wide variety of religious practices from around the world. He does not consider himself a member or representative of any particular religion. Although many see him as an enlightened being, Prabhuji has no intention of presenting himself as a preacher, guide, coach, content creator, influencer, preceptor, mentor, counselor, consultant, monitor, tutor, teacher, instructor, educator, enlightener, pedagogue, evangelist, rabbi, *posek halacha*, healer, therapist, satsangist, psychic, leader, medium, savior, or guru. In fact, Prabhuji believes spirituality is an individual, solitary, personal, private, and intimate search. It is not a collective endeavor to be undertaken through social, organized, institutional, or community religiosity.

To that end, Prabhuji does not proselytize or preach, nor does he try to persuade, convince, or make anyone change their perspective, philosophy, or religion. Others may find his insights valuable and apply them wholly or in part to their own development, but Prabhuji's teachings are not meant to be seen as personal advice, counseling, guidance, self-help methods, or techniques for spiritual, physical, emotional, or psychological development. His teachings do not promise solutions to life's spiritual, material, financial, psychological, emotional, romantic, family, social, or physical problems. Prabhuji does not offer miracles, mystical experiences, astral journeys, healings, connections with spirits, supernatural powers, or spiritual salvation.

Although he did not seek to attract followers, for 15 years (1995–2010), Prabhuji considered the requests of a few people who approached him asking to become his monastic disciples. Those who chose to see Prabhuji as their spiritual master voluntarily accepted vows of poverty and life-long dedication to spiritual practice (*sādhanā*), religious devotion (*bhakti*), and selfless service (*seva*). Prabhuji no longer accepts new disciples, but he continues to guide the small group of veteran disciples of the Ramakrishnananda Monastic Order that he founded.

Public services

Even though the monastery does not accept new residents, volunteers, donations, collaborations, or sponsorships, the public is invited to participate in daily religious services and devotional festivals at the Śrī Śrī Radha-Śyāmasundara temple.

Titles by Prabhuji

What is, as it is: Satsangs with Prabhuji (English)
ISBN-13: 978-1-945894-26-8
Lo que es, tal como es: Satsangas con Prabhuji (Spanish)
ISBN-13: 978-1-945894-27-5
Russian: ISBN-13: 978-1-945894-18-3

Kundalini yoga: The power is in you (English)
ISBN-13:978-1-945894-30-5
Kundalini yoga: El poder está en ti (Spanish)
ISBN-13:978-1-945894-31-2

Bhakti yoga: The path of love (English)
ISBN-13: 978-1-945894-28-2
Bhakti-yoga: El sendero del amor (Spanish)
ISBN-13: 978-1-945894-29-9

**Experimenting with the Truth
(English)**
ISBN-13: 978-1-945894-32-9
**Experimentando con la
Verdad (Spanish)**
ISBN-13: 978-1-945894-33-6

**Tantra: Liberation in the
world (English)**
ISBN-13: 978-1-945894-36-7
**Tantra: La liberación en el
mundo (Spanish)**
ISBN-13: 978-1-945894-37-4

**Advaita Vedanta: Being the
Self (English)**
ISBN-13: 978-1-945894-34-3
**Advaita Vedanta: Ser el Ser
(Spanish)**
ISBN-13: 978-1-945894-35-0

Īśāvāsya Upanishad
commented by Prabhuji
(English)
ISBN-13: 978-1-945894-38-1
Īśāvāsya Upaniṣad
comentado por Prabhuji
(Spanish)
ISBN-13: 978-1-945894-40-4

The Diamond Sūtra
commented by Prabhuji
(English)
ISBN-13: 978-1-945894-51-0
El Sūtra del Diamante
comentado por Prabhuji
(Spanish)
ISBN-13: 978-1-945894-54-1

I am that I am
(English)
ISBN-13: 978-1-945894-45-9
Soy el que soy
(Spanish)
ISBN-13: 978-1-945894-48-0